*I would like to express my gratitude and appr*
my vision for this book and helped in reaching the books completion. *I specifically want to thank Ronnie Schiff, Elyse Wyman, Matthew Von Doran, Dean Brown, Russel Ferante and my father E.D.C. My deepest expression of gratitude goes to my wife Anna Yanova-Cattoor for her major contributions and belief in my vision. Thank you all!*

*Sincerely,*

*Jared Cattoor*

# Contents

Answer sheets for Scale Sheet and Interval Table
on pages 110 and 111

# Introduction

The purpose of this book is to use unique puzzles to construct chords, arpeggios and scales an enjoyable, creative and abstract way. This book is perfect for beginners in music theory, high school theory students, college theory students, private instructors, professional jazz musicians, composers', professors and, essentially, all musicians. On one hand this book is about exercising your musical brain and getting you to think outside of the box. The other major factor is about learning the vocabulary of music so that you can speak the language more fluently. That said: if you do these puzzles correctly you will practically master the vocabulary. You will either engrain this information in your mind or be able to construct the vocabulary with little or no hesitation. Have you ever heard of a chord and had no idea what it was, for instance $D^\flat 7(\sharp 5)$? What are the notes in that chord? 3, 2, 1… Time's up! After you complete the puzzles in this book, come back to this page and see how easy that is to answer.

A musician must have a solid understanding of "musical vocabulary." Musical vocabulary refers to the 12 notes used in Western music andthe different combinations they can create. Notes, arpeggios, scales and chords are the foundational vocabulary that makes up the language of music. All of those elements turn into lines, licks, chord progressions, melodies and other ideas that create music and songs. Just like letters combine to create a word, notes played simultaneously make a chord. Words together create a sentence, just like notes together create a melody. Hopefully, those examples give you some understanding and get you thinking. Music is truly a language. The better you understand it, the better you will play.

This book contains the most common vocabulary used in popular music. The puzzles will "test" your understanding of the vocab and help ensure you are really on top of the info! They will challenge your thinking, no matter how basic or advanced your theory knowledge is. It is very important that musicians really understand how to spell chords and scales without hesitation. That is exactly what you will be able to do after going through this book.

This is a book for the brain, but remember, that without applying this information to your instrument, there is no music...

• Each one of the chords, arpeggios and scale types allow for a whole world of music.

• Each sound can be breathtaking and wonderful.

• Spend some time experimenting with each interval, chord, arpeggio and scale presented in this book.

• Sing the notes and play them on your instrument.

• Do one page at a time and play everything on each page to check your "answers". Really listen to what the chord, arpeggio or scale sounds like so when you paint your mural, you know what colors you have to use.


### For the total beginner:

This book may move a bit fast if you have zero experience playing or with music theory. Just take it one page at a time and really soak in the information. You can use it for the rest of your life, so there is no need to rush. Make sure to complete all of the "exercises" in Part I. If you're having trouble understanding the information in this book, it may be helpful to get a private instructor who knows theory well to help you use this book and learn music theory.

### For the intermediate player:

This book is perfect for you! If you are learning music theory and still stuck in some areas or confused on what notes are in an A7sus4 chord, for example... These puzzles will help you fill in the gaps and you will master spelling this musical vocabulary. It is such an important tool for all musicians when reading music, playing chord charts, improvising and simply speaking the language of music.

When you master these puzzles, your musical mind will expand very fast and you will get a much deeper and complex understanding of music vocabulary.

### For the professionals:

If you are a theory professor, jazz musician, private teacher or professional player of any kind, these puzzles will challenge you to stay at the top of your mental game! These puzzles are great teaching tools. They've been used with many students, and this method produces amazing results!

# Part I
# THE FOUNDATION

If you already know advanced chord and scale construction, please feel to jump ahead to page 38 and read "How the Puzzles Work."

In the first part of the book you will learn the necessary building blocks to understand simple music theory and complete the puzzles. There are descriptions of each element along with exercises. If you are new to theory, this book will be an outstanding way to really learn and retain this information. Here are the basic elements in the language.

# The Musical Alphabet - Notes and the Keyboard

The very first thing you must understand is the musical alphabet. The alphabet is the collection of individual notes in music. The musical alphabet consists of the first 7 letters of the Latin alphabet; we use A B C D E F G to name the notes in music. The alphabet moves in a circle and repeats itself. That means, the letter that comes after G is A. Not all music starts from A though. In fact, it can start from any of the notes. The alphabet should be learned forward and backwards starting from any note. Read alloud each row below to get started.

| Forward | | | | | | | |
|---|---|---|---|---|---|---|---|
| A | B | C | D | E | F | G | A |
| B | C | D | E | F | G | A | B |
| C | D | E | F | G | A | B | C |
| D | E | F | G | A | B | C | D |
| E | F | G | A | B | C | D | E |
| F | G | A | B | C | D | E | F |
| G | A | B | C | D | E | F | G |

| Backward | | | | | | | |
|---|---|---|---|---|---|---|---|
| A | G | F | E | D | C | B | A |
| B | A | G | F | E | D | C | B |
| C | B | A | G | F | E | D | C |
| D | C | B | A | G | F | E | D |
| E | D | C | B | A | G | F | E |
| F | E | D | C | B | A | G | F |
| G | F | E | D | C | B | A | G |

It is important to learn the notes very well. It may be a little strange saying the alphabet backward, but you will get used to it quickly if you do it often.

Now, fill in the following chart one row at a time as printed in the previous one. This will reinforce your memory and understanding of the alphabet.

Forward                                              Backward

A   B _ _ _ _ _ _ _                                  A   G _ _ _ _ _ _ _

B   C _ _ _ _ _ _ _                                  B   A _ _ _ _ _ _ _

C _ _ _ _ _ _ _                                      C _ _ _ _ _ _ _

D _ _ _ _ _ _ _                                      D _ _ _ _ _ _ _

E _ _ _ _ _ _ _                                      E _ _ _ _ _ _ _

F _ _ _ _ _ _ _                                      F _ _ _ _ _ _ _

G _ _ _ _ _ _ _                                      G _ _ _ _ _ _ _

Now, play and sing (simultaneously) each row using your instrument. Listen to the sound of each sequence of notes. Each sequence has its own unique sound. Note: If you do now know where the notes are on your instrument you must learn now. I also recommend saying the alphabet forward and backward from different notes in your free time. Spend some time doing this until you are very confident with the notes.

A–G are the main note names, but there are five more notes in Western music — there are sharps and flats. So in total, the musical alphabet consists of 12 notes. That's pretty amazing if you think about it. Almost all the music you have ever heard is a combination of only 12 notes! In fact, most of the time only seven of them or fewer are used. Now, take a look at the keyboard to see where the notes are.

# The Keyboard

Every musician should understand how a piano works. The keyboard has the best visual reference for the notes in music. It is okay if you don't play the piano, but you should learn about it. Knowing the keyboard layout and the functions of a piano can help you understand your instrument and all of music on a higher level. There is a keyboard on every puzzle page to help you through the puzzles, if needed.

The notes A—G make up all of the white keys on a piano, and the other five notes make up the black keys. Look at the keyboard and see where the notes are placed on the keyboard. Memorize where just one note is, and you can easily find the others. C is normally the first note shown to anyone, so lets find C.

The black keys alternate in pairs of two and three, leaving a space in between each pair. C is directly to the left of the black key that is in the pair of two as noted in the following keyboard diagram.

The white keys (including C) are called the "natural" notes. They are the letter names of the alphabet. The keys go in the order of the musical alphabet. So if you start on C the very next note is D... then E, F, G, A, B back to C and the cycle continues until the end of the keyboard.

The black keys are the sharps or flats. There is a black key in-between every white key **except** for **two pairs** of notes: there is **not** a black key between the notes **B and C**, and the notes **E and F**. It is very important that you memorize this immediately! Look at the keyboard and see for yourself— B-C and E-F do not have a black key in-between them!

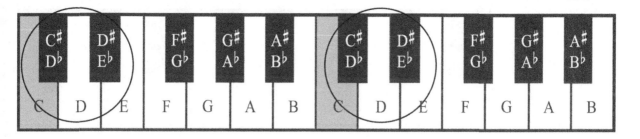

The white keys (including C) are called the "natural" notes. They are the letter names of the alphabet. The keys go in the order of the musical alphabet. So if you start on C the very next note is D... then E, F, G, A, B back to C and the cycle repeats until the end of the keyboard.

The black keys are the sharps or flats. There is a black key in-between every white key except for two pairs of notes: there is not a black key between the notes B and C, and the notes E and F. It is very important that you memorize this immediately! Look at the keyboard and see for yourself— B-C and E-F do not have a black key in-between them.

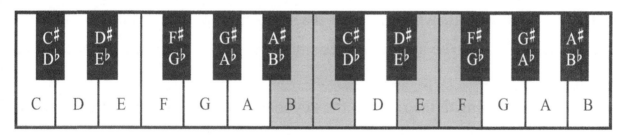

## Half and Whole Steps

A "half step" is the distance from one key to the very next key on the keyboard. A "whole step" is the distance of two half steps. The following illustration gives two examples of different positions of half and whole steps.

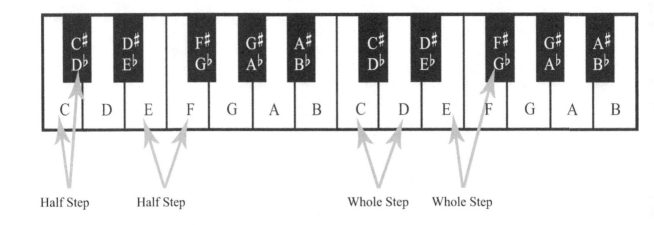

# Accidentals

Now to address the five remaining notes: An "accidental" is a sign used to raise or lower the pitch of a note. By using "accidentals," a natural note will also add the name "sharp" or "flat" to a note letter. For example: D sharp or D flat. The symbols are used to indicate whether a note is a sharp or a flat. The symbol used to indicate a sharp is ♯, and the symbol representing a flat is ♭. You can see them on the black keys above.

When going to the right on the keyboard, the black key is called the sharp of the white key before it. When going to the left, the black key is called the flat of the white key before it. So black keys can have two names. Look at the black key in-between A and B to understand the concept. That key says A♯ and B♭ — it can be either.

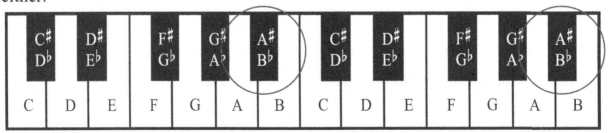

This key can be called A$\sharp$, since it is a half step above A. It can also be called B$\flat$, since it is a half step below B.

Review: There are 7 "letter names" in the alphabet right? Each letter name can be changed to a sharp, and each can become a flat.

**Natural**: A - B - C - D - E - F - G - A
**Sharp**:  A$\sharp$ - B$\sharp$ - C$\sharp$ - D$\sharp$ - E$\sharp$ - F$\sharp$ - G$\sharp$ - A$\sharp$
**Flats**: A$\flat$ - B$\flat$ - C$\flat$ - D$\flat$ - E$\flat$ - F$\flat$ - G$\flat$ - A$\flat$

You might be thinking, "That's more than 12 notes." There are 21 different ways to "spell" the notes as written above, but if you count the notes on the keyboard from A to A there are only 12. You have the option of "altering" the spellings. When saying the note names ascending (going up in pitch, or to the right of the keyboard) using sharps you get: A, A$\sharp$, B, C, C$\sharp$, D, D$\sharp$, E, F, F$\sharp$, G, G$\sharp$ and back to A. If you descend (moving down in pitch, or to the left of the keyboard) using flats you get: A, A$\flat$, G, G$\flat$, F, E, E$\flat$, D, D$\flat$, C, B, B$\flat$ and A.

Remember that B – C and E – F do not have a black note in between them. B goes directly to C and E goes directly to F. The same idea applies when descending. That is how the *chromatic scale* is spelled. The *chromatic scale* uses all 12 notes in order and can start from any note.

Practice saying the alphabet forward and backwards using all 12 notes (chromatically) just like you did with the natural notes. Here's the example:

### Forward

A - A$\sharp$ - B - C - C$\sharp$ - D - D$\sharp$ - E - F - F$\sharp$ - G - G$\sharp$ - A
B - C - C$\sharp$ - D - D$\sharp$ - E - F - F$\sharp$ - G - G$\sharp$ - A - A$\sharp$ - B
C - C$\sharp$ - D - D$\sharp$ - E - F - F$\sharp$ - G - G$\sharp$ - A - A$\sharp$ - B - C, etc…

## Backward

A - A♭ - G - G♭ - F - E - E♭ - D - D♭ - C - B - B♭ - A

G - G♭ - F - E - E♭ - D - D♭ - C - B - B♭ - A - A♭ - G

F - E - E♭ - D - D♭ - C - B - B♭ - A - A♭ - G - G♭ - F, etc…

Now, fill in the following chart one row at a time just as you did with the natural notes on page 9.

## Forward

*A*   *A#* __ __ __ __ __ __ __ __ __

*B* __ __ __ __ __ __ __ __ __

__ __ __ __ __ __ __ __ __

__ __ __ __ __ __ __ __ __

__ __ __ __ __ __ __ __ __

__ __ __ __ __ __ __ __ __

__ __ __ __ __ __ __ __ __

## Bakcward

*A*   *A♭* __ __ __ __ __ __ __ __ __

*G* __ __ __ __ __ __ __ __ __

__ __ __ __ __ __ __ __ __

__ __ __ __ __ __ __ __ __

__ __ __ __ __ __ __ __ __

__ __ __ __ __ __ __ __ __

__ __ __ __ __ __ __ __ __

Once again, play and sing each row forward and backwards. Also, make your own "definition"/interpretation of what the Chromatic Scale sounds like to you. Does this sound remind you of anything? Can you attach an image or emotion to this sound? Answering these questions will help you internalize and remember this specific sound. Do this process for all new information you learn in this book to get maximum benefits.

At this point you should understand all 12 of the notes in the Western music scale. Congratulations! Spend some time saying, writing, and singing and playing the chromatic scale forward and backwards before moving on.

# Intervals

An interval is simply the distance between two notes. Numbers are used to identify the distances. Let's start with generic intervals.

There are 7 letter names in the musical alphabet, and there are 8 numbers used to define basic intervals. The distances are called: *prime, seconds, thirds, fourths, fifths, sixths, sevenths* and *"octaves"*. A note by itself is sometimes called a "prime" interval. A note that a chord or scale is named after can be described as the "root" interval; root means the starting point. An example is F Major. The note F is the "root" of the chord.

Interval numbers equals the distance between two notes. For example: A to C is a third: A, B, C = 1, 2, 3 notes. This concept works the same for all intervals.

On the next page are three examples of each type of generic interval. Take some time to count the distances between each set of intervals below. Make sure you understand why each interval is named what it is. Actually count how many letter names occur between the notes. For example: C D E F = 1 2 3 4. F is a fourth away from C. Do all the examples below.

**Prime or (Unison)**: A - A,   C - C,   F - F

**Seconds**: A - B,   C - D,   F - G

**Thirds**: A - C,   C - E,   F - A

**Fourths**: A - D,   C - F,   F - B

**Fifths**: A - E,   C - G,   F - C

**Sixths**: A - F,   C - A,   F - D

**Sevenths**: A - G,   C - B,   F - E

**Eighths or (Octave)**: A - A,   C - C,   F - F

Now that you have a feel for generic intervals, let's learn about <u>specific intervals</u>.

First, specific intervals are measured by *half steps*. There are five types of specific intervals. They are: *perfect, major, minor, augmented* and *diminished*. These names are added to the number of the interval, such as "perfect fourth" or "minor third".

The following page has a list of the interval types, the interval formula to create the specific interval, and a few examples of each interval. Study each one carefully. Use the diagram to reference the examples and see them on the keyboard.

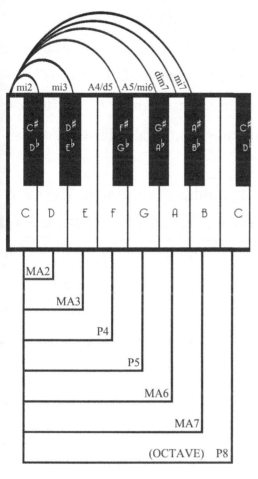

| Interval name | Interval "formula" | Note name |
|---|---|---|
| Prime (root) | Static | C |
| Minor 2nd | 1 half step | C - D♭ |
| Major 2nd | 2 half steps | C - D |
| Minor 3rd | 3 half steps | C - E♭ |
| Major 3rd | 4 half steps | C - E |
| Perfect 4th | 5 half steps | C - F |
| Augmented 4th | 6 half steps | C - F♯ |
| Diminished 5th | 6 half steps | C - G♭ |
| Perfect 5th | 7 half steps | C - G |
| Augmented 5th | 8 half steps | C - G♯ |
| Minor 6th | 8 half steps | C - A♭ |
| Major 6th | 9 half steps | C - A |
| Diminished 7th | 9 half steps | C - B♭♭ |
| Minor 7th | 10 half steps | C - B♭ |
| Major 7th | 11 half steps | C - B |
| Perfect 8th (Octave) | 12 half steps | C - C |

Key: R = Root,  m = Minor,  M = Major,  A = Augmented,  D = Diminished,  8ve = Octave

You may have noticed some "enharmonic equivalents." An *enharmonic equivalent* is the same pitch spelled differently, for example A♭ and G♯. They are musical synonyms. There are three pairs of intervals that can create enharmonic equivalents:

- Augmented 4th/diminished 5th,
- Augmented 5th/minor 6th and
- Major 6th/diminished 7th are the pairs.

17

The correct spelling of these intervals is very important. Notice the augmented 4th is spelled F$\sharp$ and the diminished 5th is spelled G$\flat$. They are the same sound, but the augmented 4th is spelled as F$\sharp$ because F is the 4th letter from C: C – D – E – F (1 – 2 – 3 – 4). The same goes for the diminished 5th. G is the 5th note from C. The concept *always* applies when talking about intervals. That should explain the augmented 5th and minor 6th too.

The concept also applies to the 7th's. The diminished 7th may seem confusing: The interval of a diminished 7th is a "double flatted" 7th. That means a major 7th is "flatted" twice: B to B$\flat$ to B$\flat\flat$. There are both double flatted or double sharped notes. Here is the symbol for double sharp: $\times$ The symbol for a double flat is two flat symbols together. B$\flat\flat$ is enharmonic to A. A$\times$ is enharmonic to B. You can do that with any note. It is possible to have each of the seven letter names spelled as a double sharp or double flat.

Double accidentals are rare and may seem impractical, but they do exist. In fact, you will encounter many while doing the puzzles.


Congratulations on getting through the intervals! All of the information above may seem like a lot if you have never seen it before. It's important to read it carefully and do the work. *[Remember, if it is a bit challenging, you can always e-mail me at jaredcattoor@gmail.com to tutor you, or find a local music teacher.]*

# Spelling Intervals

You have made it to your first interactive challenge! Now, you're prepared to create the intervals yourself! The examples on page 15 all start from C, so now A-G have been added for you. Use the "interval formula" on page 17 to create the intervals. There will be a reminder at the side of every row for you. The first column is done for you as an example to make sure you understand how this works. Follow the formula to get the answer. For example: If the problem is MA6 and the "root" is A, then you know to go up chromatically 9 half steps to get there (unless you figure out a faster way): A, A♯, B, C, C♯, D, D♯, E, F, F♯.... 1 2 3 4 5 6 7 8 9. F♯ is a MA6th away from A. It's that easy. Look at a keyboard if that helps.

## Fill in the empty spaces!

| | | | | | | | | |
|---|---|---|---|---|---|---|---|---|
| (1 HS) mi2 | A - $B^\flat$ | B - ___ | C - ___ | D - ___ | E - ___ | F - ___ | G - ___ | A - ___ |
| (2 HS) MA2 | B - $C^\sharp$ | C - ___ | D - ___ | E - ___ | F - ___ | G - ___ | A - ___ | B - ___ |
| (3 HS) mi3 | C - $E^\flat$ | D - ___ | E - ___ | F - ___ | G - ___ | A - ___ | B - ___ | C - ___ |
| (4 HS) MA3 | D - $F^\sharp$ | E - ___ | F - ___ | G - ___ | A - ___ | B - ___ | C - ___ | D - ___ |
| (5 HS) P4 | E - $A$ | F - ___ | G - ___ | A - ___ | B - ___ | C - ___ | D - ___ | E - ___ |
| (6 HS) A4 | F - $B$ | G - ___ | A - ___ | B - ___ | C - ___ | D - ___ | E - ___ | F - ___ |
| (6 HS) dim5 | G - $D^\flat$ | A - ___ | B - ___ | C - ___ | D - ___ | E - ___ | F - ___ | G - ___ |
| (7 HS) P5 | A - $E$ | B - ___ | C - ___ | D - ___ | E - ___ | F - ___ | G - ___ | A - ___ |
| (8 HS) A5 | B - $F^\times$ | C - ___ | D - ___ | E - ___ | F - ___ | G - ___ | A - ___ | B - ___ |
| (8 HS) mi6 | C - $A^\flat$ | D - ___ | E - ___ | F - ___ | G - ___ | A - ___ | B - ___ | C - ___ |
| (9 HS) MA6 | D - $B$ | E - ___ | F - ___ | G - ___ | A - ___ | B - ___ | C - ___ | D - ___ |
| (9 HS) dim7 | E - $D^\flat$ | F - ___ | G - ___ | A - ___ | B - ___ | C - ___ | D - ___ | E - ___ |
| (10 HS) mi7 | F - $E^\flat$ | G - ___ | A - ___ | B - ___ | C - ___ | D - ___ | E - ___ | F - ___ |
| (11 HS) MA7 | G - $F^\sharp$ | A - ___ | B - ___ | C - ___ | D - ___ | E - ___ | F - ___ | G - ___ |
| (12 HS) P8 | A - $A$ | B - ___ | C - ___ | D - ___ | E - ___ | F - ___ | G - ___ | A - ___ |

Check the back of the book to see an answer sheet. Make sure you are doing it right. You must understand the intervals to do the rest of this book! Also recommended: Play and sing each of the intervals to hear what they sound like.

# The Major Scale!

The major scale is the most commonly used scale in Western music. The major scale is also known as the *Ionian mode* when referring to the diatonic modes. The scale is made up of seven notes and the octave. *Solfège*, or numbers are often used to refer to the specific scale degrees. The numbers are 1, 2, 3, 4, 5, 6, 7, (8)— 8 is the *octave.* The corresponding solfège is: Do, Re, Mi, Fa, Sol, La, Ti, (Do). The numbers and solfège can be applied to any of the scales. There are 12 pitches in music; so there can only be 12 major scales. If *enharmonic* notes are used, you can have more than 12 spellings. For example: C♯ major and D♭ major are *enharmonic* to each other, but spelled totally different. Some spellings are more practical than others due to the amount of sharps and flats. For example, the key of C♯ major has 7 sharps—everything is sharp! D♭ major has only 5 flats. D♭ is used more often since it has less accidentals.

Now, you're ready to learn the building blocks of the major scale and start to build!

There are two ways of thinking to create a major scale: One way to create the scale is to use whole steps and half steps. The other way to create the scale is to use only half steps.

The "major scale formula" is <u>W</u>hole step, <u>W</u>hole step, <u>H</u>alf step, <u>W</u>hole step, <u>W</u>hole step, <u>W</u>hole step, <u>H</u>alf step. Think 2 wholes and a half, and 3 wholes and

The notes in the C major scale are C D E F G A B C. C major is the only major (Ionian) scale that doesn't contain sharps or flats. When using the formula, the steps are applied after the root.

| | | | | |
|---|---|---|---|---|
| W | C - D is a whole step | | 2 | C - D is 2 half steps |
| W | D - E is a whole step | | 2 | D - E is 2 half steps |
| H | E - F is a half step | | 1 | E - F is 1 half step |
| W | F - G is a whole step | | 2 | F - G is 2 half steps |
| W | G - A is a whole step | | 2 | G - A is 2 half steps |
| W | A - B is a whole step | | 2 | A - B is 2 half steps |
| H | B - C is a half step | | 1 | B - C is 1 half step |

Use whichever formula is easiest for you. The formula W, W, H, W, W, W, H is on the scale sheet for you, but if you want to think in half steps that's fine too. Here are a few more scale examples to make sure you understand how they're constructed before you write them on your own.

### E♭ major scale

The notes are E♭, F, G, A♭, B♭, C, D, E♭. Notice that there are 3 flats in the key of E♭ major.

| | |
|---|---|
| E♭ - F | 1 whole step or 2 half steps. |
| F - G | 1 whole step or 2 half steps. |
| G - A♭ | 1 half step. ← Notice G went to A♭ and not A. A would have been a whole step. |
| A♭ - B♭ | 1 whole step or 2 half steps. |
| B♭ - C | 1 whole step or 2 half steps. |
| C - D | 1 whole step or 2 half steps. |
| D - E♭ | 1 half step. |

The number of sharps or flats a key has is important to memorize and know. The *Circle of Fifths* (on page 30) will explain more on that.

Here's one more key before you get to build a scale yourself. This example includes the scale degree number, the solfège and the note name!

### D Major scale

D major has two sharps in the key: F$\sharp$ and C$\sharp$.

| | |
|---|---|
| 1/Do | D – E is 1 whole step or 2 half steps. |
| 2/Re | E – F$\sharp$ is 1 whole step or 2 half steps. |
| 3/Mi | F$\sharp$ – G is 1 half step. |
| 4/Fa | G – A is 1 whole step or 2 half steps. |
| 5/Sol | A – B is 1 whole step or 2 half steps. |
| 6/La | B – C$\sharp$ is 1 whole step or 2 half steps. |
| 7/Ti | C$\sharp$ – D is one half step. |

Remember there is no half step in-between E and F, so a whole step from E is F$\sharp$. Check the keyboard as a reference.

This is just like E and F. Again there's no half step in-between B and C; so if you ascend a whole step from B you are taken to C$\sharp$.

Time to move onto your next challenge! Writing out the major scales!

# Spelling the Major Scale

The sheet on the next page has 15 major scale possibilities on it. Write out the scales using the formulas at the top of the page. The solfège scale degrees (numbers) and formula are above the scale for you to use. The keyboard is also on every puzzle page for a reference. Fill in the correct note names directly under the formula. Use the formula to get each individual note of the scale. The first scale is done for you as an example.

### Review:

• Each major scale will always use all seven letters of the alphabet (A-G).

- There should never be two of the same letters in a major scale.
- Example: A to A♯ would be incorrect. You must always move to the next letter: A to B♭ would be correct.
- There will never be a sharp and a flat in the same major scale. If any of that occurs, no worries, just re-do the scale and fix the mistake.

**Fill in each major scale using the formula W W H W W W H.**

| Do | Re | Mi | Fa | Sol | La | Ti | (Do) |
|----|----|----|----|----|----|----|----|
| 1 | 2 | 3 | 4 | 5 | 6 | 7 | (8) |
| R | W | W | H | W | W | W | H |
| C | D | E | F | G | A | B | C |
| G | | | | | | | |
| D | | | | | | | |
| A | | | | | | | |
| E | | | | | | | |
| B | | | | | | | |
| F♯ | | | | | | | |
| C♯ | | | | | | | |
| F | | | | | | | |
| B♭ | | | | | | | |
| E♭ | | | | | | | |
| A♭ | | | | | | | |
| D♭ | | | | | | | |
| G♭ | | | | | | | |
| C♭ | | | | | | | |

Congratulations on writing out the major scale.

It's important to make sure you really understand how to build these scales. The goal is to get to a point where you can quickly and easily construct any major scale with little or no hesitation. If this is the first time you have done all of the scales on this sheet, you should probably repeat the process at least five times — it really requires repetition. Do this enough and you'll memorize all of the scales. That'll be great for your playing, because you'll always know what key you're in, and you won't have to fumble around listening to hit a "right" note. You'll know where they all are without thinking. Knowing the notes of any major scale will help you play so much music.

Please do this sheet 5 times before moving to the next section. It will make the puzzles much easier. It is also recommended to try teaching someone else how to do these. Show them the same method. Teaching is one of the best ways to see what you really know, and it helps you learn faster than ever. After writing the scales out, play each of them and listen to what they sound like.

| Do | Re | Mi | Fa | Sol | La | Ti | (Do) |
|----|----|----|----|-----|----|----|------|
| 1 | 2 | 3 | 4 | 5 | 6 | 7 | (8) |
| R | W | W | H | W | W | W | H |
| C | D | E | F | G | A | B | C |
| G | | | | | | | |
| D | | | | | | | |
| A | | | | | | | |
| E | | | | | | | |
| B | | | | | | | |
| F# | | | | | | | |
| C# | | | | | | | |
| F | | | | | | | |
| Bb | | | | | | | |
| Eb | | | | | | | |
| Ab | | | | | | | |
| Db | | | | | | | |
| Gb | | | | | | | |
| Cb | | | | | | | |

| Do | Re | Mi | Fa | Sol | La | Ti | (Do) |
|----|----|----|----|-----|----|----|------|
| 1 | 2 | 3 | 4 | 5 | 6 | 7 | (8) |
| R | W | W | H | W | W | W | H |
| C | D | E | F | G | A | B | C |
| G | | | | | | | |
| D | | | | | | | |
| A | | | | | | | |
| E | | | | | | | |
| B | | | | | | | |
| F$^\sharp$ | | | | | | | |
| C$^\sharp$ | | | | | | | |
| F | | | | | | | |
| B$^\flat$ | | | | | | | |
| E$^\flat$ | | | | | | | |
| A$^\flat$ | | | | | | | |
| D$^\flat$ | | | | | | | |
| G$^\flat$ | | | | | | | |
| C$^\flat$ | | | | | | | |

| Do | Re | Mi | Fa | Sol | La | Ti | (Do) |
|----|----|----|----|-----|----|----|------|
| 1 | 2 | 3 | 4 | 5 | 6 | 7 | (8) |
| R | W | W | H | W | W | W | H |
| C | D | E | F | G | A | B | C |
| G | | | | | | | |
| D | | | | | | | |
| A | | | | | | | |
| E | | | | | | | |
| B | | | | | | | |
| F# | | | | | | | |
| C# | | | | | | | |
| F | | | | | | | |
| B♭ | | | | | | | |
| E♭ | | | | | | | |
| A♭ | | | | | | | |
| D♭ | | | | | | | |
| G♭ | | | | | | | |
| C♭ | | | | | | | |

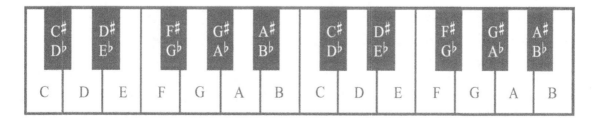

| Do | Re | Mi | Fa | Sol | La | Ti | (Do) |
|---|---|---|---|---|---|---|---|
| 1 | 2 | 3 | 4 | 5 | 6 | 7 | (8) |
| R | W | W | H | W | W | W | H |
| C | D | E | F | G | A | B | C |
| G | | | | | | | |
| D | | | | | | | |
| A | | | | | | | |
| E | | | | | | | |
| B | | | | | | | |
| F# | | | | | | | |
| C# | | | | | | | |
| F | | | | | | | |
| B♭ | | | | | | | |
| E♭ | | | | | | | |
| A♭ | | | | | | | |
| D♭ | | | | | | | |
| G♭ | | | | | | | |
| C♭ | | | | | | | |

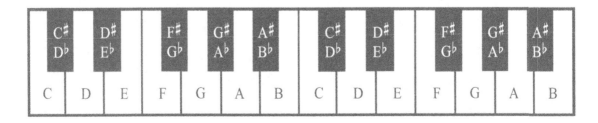

Congratulations! You have made it to the last page of scales! At this point, you should be becoming very familiar with the scales. Try timing yourself on this one and see how fast you can do it. The time to beat is three minutes! That may seem easy… or it may seem crazy! With repetition, you will be able to do this with ease.

| Do | Re | Mi | Fa | Sol | La | Ti | (Do) |
|----|----|----|----|-----|----|----|------|
| 1 | 2 | 3 | 4 | 5 | 6 | 7 | (8) |
| R | W | W | H | W | W | W | H |
| C | D | E | F | G | A | B | C |
| G | | | | | | | |
| D | | | | | | | |
| A | | | | | | | |
| E | | | | | | | |
| B | | | | | | | |
| F♯ | | | | | | | |
| C♯ | | | | | | | |
| F | | | | | | | |
| B♭ | | | | | | | |
| E♭ | | | | | | | |
| A♭ | | | | | | | |
| D♭ | | | | | | | |
| G♭ | | | | | | | |
| C♭ | | | | | | | |

# The Circle of Fifths!
## (aka The Circle of fourths)

The circle of fifths is a huge part of Western music theory. It is not necessary for you to understand the circle to do the puzzles, but it can be very helpful. The circle of fifths was created to display how many sharps or flats each key has in it. The cycle is often described with a clock-like picture similar to the one below. Look at the picture and you will notice that C is at 12 o'clock with the number 0 under it. The numbers represent how many accidentals are in each key. C is the only key with 0 accidentals in it.

Go clockwise on the circle and the next letter you see is G. That is because G is the 5th note in the C scale. The circle moves clockwise in *perfect fifths* all the way around the circle.

Now, notice the number 1 by G. The key of G major has one sharp (F$\sharp$) The next letter moving clockwise from G is D. D is the 5th note in the key of G; D major has two sharps (F$\sharp$ and C$\sharp$). Each key always adds one accidental and always keeps the previous accidentals. When you move clockwise, you will have sharp keys until C$\sharp$. If you go counterclockwise, you have flats until C$\flat$. Also, if you move counterclockwise, the interval from note to note is a *perfect fourth*. You could also call this the "Cycle of Fourths." When moving counterclockwise, the keys move in perfect fourths. Notice that C to F is a perfect forth and so on. Notice that the major scale exercises are set up using the circle of fifths for the sharp keys and the cycle of fourths for the flat keys.

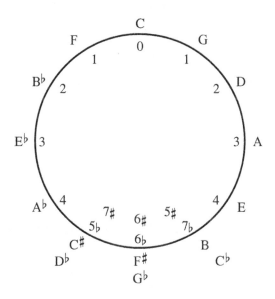

# Chord/Arpeggio Construction!

This is it! After you understand this, you're prepared for the puzzles and so much more with your life in music.

A *chord* is made up of three or more notes played simultaneously. An *arpeggio* is simply a chord that is played or sung in sequence, so the notes are played one at a time instead of simultaneously. The most basic type of chord is called a *triad*. A triad is chord with three notes in it. There are four basic triads: *major, minor, augmented* and *diminished*. You have learned about all of these types of intervals. Now, just add one more note to create a chord. As follows are a few ways to construct chords that are easy and practical. To do this though, you should be thoroughly comfortable, building the major scale and intervals. Make sure you have done the interval and scale sheets prior to this section before moving on.

All chords can be related to the major scale. All chords except "sus" chords have some type of 1st (Root), 3rd and 5th construction. (Sus chords don't contain a

3rd in them.) Use the major scale to build chords.

The C major chord has the notes C E G in it.

• The C major scale is spelled C D E F G A B C.

• Take the 1st, 3rd and 5th scale degrees and you have the notes that create a C major chord! C E G = 1 3 5 of the C major scale.

Here's another example: The D major chord has the notes D, F$\sharp$ and A.

• The D major scale has the notes D E F$\sharp$ G A B C$\sharp$ and D.

• The 1st is D, the 3rd is F$\sharp$ and the 5th scale degree is A. There's your chord.

You can use this same approach to make all the other chord types as well by simply altering the notes according to the chord formula. Here's the A major chord and each basic triad.

• The A major scale is A, B, C$\sharp$, D, E, F$\sharp$, G$\sharp$, A.

• The A major chord is spelled: A, C$\sharp$, E — the 1st, 3rd and 5th notes in the scale.

• The A minor chord is spelled: A, C, E. Notice C is natural. C is lowered one half step because the minor chord formula is 1, b3, 5. The b3 tells you to lower the 3rd by a half step.

• The A augmented chord is spelled: A, C$\sharp$, E$\sharp$. The formula for augmented chords is 1, 3, $\sharp$5, so the 5th is raised one half step to E$\sharp$. The A diminished chord is spelled: A, C, E$\flat$: The chord formula for diminished chords is 1, $\flat$3, $\flat$5. The 3rd and 5th are lowered one half step for diminished.

All of the chords can be built by using this approach. There are many different types of chords. You can always relate them to the major scale and make the alterations to spell the chords if you like that method. Take a look at all the chord types on the next page. Onthe next page is a graph with all of the chord/arpeggio

32

types that are in this book.

| Chord Type | Chord Formula | Corresponding Interval Distances |
|---|---|---|
| *Major Chords* | | |
| Major | 1 3 5 | $R\,M^3\,m^3$ |
| Major6 | 1 3 5 6 | $R\,M^3\,m^3\,M^2$ |
| Major7 | 1 3 5 7 | $R\,M^3\,m^3\,M^3$ |
| Major add2 | 1 2 3 5 | $R\,M^2\,M^2\,m^3$ |
| Minor Chords | | |
| Minor | 1 $\flat$3 5 | $R\,m^3\,M^3$ |
| Minor6 | 1 $\flat$3 5 6 | $R\,m^3\,M^3\,M^2$ |
| Minor7 | 1 $\flat$3 5 $\flat$7 | $R\,m^3\,M^3\,m^3$ |
| Minor add2 | 1 2 $\flat$3 5 | $R\,M^2\,m^2\,M^3$ |
| Minor Major 7 | 1 $\flat$3 5 7 | $R\,m^3\,P^5\,M^7$ |
| Dominant Chords | | |
| Dominant7 | 1 3 5 $\flat$7 | $R\,M^3\,m^3\,m^3$ |
| Dom7 sus4 | 1 4 5 $\flat$7 | $R\,P^4\,M^2\,m^3$ |
| Diminished Chords | | |
| Diminished | 1 $\flat$3 $\flat$5 | $R\,m^3\,m^3$ |
| Diminished 7 | 1 $\flat$3 $\flat$5 $\flat\flat$7 | $R\,m^3\,m^3\,m^3$ |
| Minor7 $\flat$5 | 1 $\flat$3 $\flat$5 $\flat$7 | $R\,m^3\,d^5\,m^7$ |
| Augmented Chords | | |
| Augmented | 1 3 $\sharp$5 | $R\,M^3\,M^3$ |
| Augmented7 | 1 3 $\sharp$5 $\flat$7 | $R\,M^3\,M^3\,M^2$ |
| Suspended Chords | | |
| Sus2 | 1 2 5 | $R\,M^2\,P^4$ |
| Sus4 | 1 4 5 | $R\,P^4\,M^2$ |

So, this may look like a lot of chords and you may feel a bit over-whelmed. No worries. Just learn one at a time at your pace.

There are other options for constructing the chords: One is using the major scale and then altering notes to fit the formula like what's shown before. The other option is to strictly use the intervals that create the chord. There is often a mix between the two methods, but choose what works best for you.

In this book, you will be constructing all of those chord types from any given root. You will also become a "master" of spelling chords and scales after going through the puzzles. Most importantly, you will be able to easily create all of these chords and arpeggios on your instrument.

### More About Chord Construction

The object of this book is to show you a way to construct chords/arpeggios and scales from any note of the chord.

• That said, most of the puzzles do not start from the root of the chord.

• The puzzle will give you the note A for example, and tell you that A is the third of a major chord.

• Now it's your job to figure out what the rest of the notes in the chord are.

Time to do that using the interval approach:

**Here's the example: 1, 3, 5 = \_\_\_\_, A, \_\_\_\_**

If you look at the chord table on **page 33**, you can use the third column to answer this question. For a major chord, the interval distances are R, M3, m3. Given this information, you can find the notes of the chord easily. It means that if

34

you have the root, then the 3rd is a major third up from that, and the fifth is a minor third up from the 3rd.

So in your current example, A is the 3rd. All you have to do is use the interval distances to get the answer. To get the root, go down a major 3rd interval (four half steps) — A, A♭, G, G♭ and F — the root is F. To get the 5th, just go up a minor third from A (three half steps) — A, A♯, B, and C. C is the 5th. The chord is F major.

There is a diagram for each type of chord before each puzzle for you to reference. They have all of the information you need. Here is an example of one.

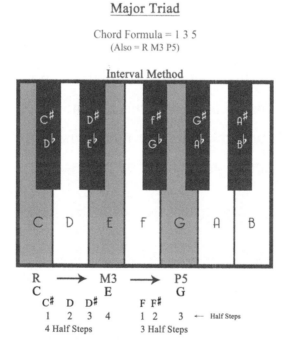

As you can see, all of the information is provided.

Here is a 4 note chord example; 1, b3, 5, 6 = _____, _____, B, _____

This is a minor 6th chord. B is the 5th. If you look at minor sixth chords in the table, you will see the corresponding interval distances in the formula are R, m3, M3, M2. If you do as the formula says and go up a major 2nd (two half steps) from B, you get C♯ as the 6th — B, C, C♯ is two half steps. If you go down a major 3rd interval (four half steps) from B, you get the ♭3 of the chord. B, B♭, A, A♭, and G makes four half steps. Lastly, you must go down a minor 3rd from G to get the root—G, G♭, F, E. E is the root: E, G, B, C♯ make up a E minor 6th chord.

Here's another potential thought process using the scale approach. You are given B as your 5th. You know an unaltered 5th of a chord is an interval of a perfect 5th. Just go down a perfect fifth to get the root, and then relate to the major scale of the root and make the alterations.

Anyway you can figure out how to spell the chords will be fine. Just make sure you're solid on building scales and intervals, and the chords should come easily. If you're having trouble understanding, you may wish to find a private teacher. Not many people learn this information totally by themselves.

Part II
# TRIAD CHORD PUZZLE

## How the chord puzzles work.

• Each puzzle is made out of a grid box.

• The boxes are made out of equal rows and columns.

• You will solve each chord one row at a time.

• All puzzles in this book are to be solved horizontally.

• Each row has the same letter in it, but in a different column. (The diagonal line has no significance other that organization)

• The row gives a fixed note, and the column represents the chord tone that the note is assigned.

• The chord tones at the top of each column define the quality of the chord

Your job is to figure out the remaining chord tones in each row, one row at a time. The following grid is an example of a major chord puzzle. The columns read R (root), 3 (major 3rd) and 5 (perfect 5th). Those are the chord tones that create a major triad.

|  R  |  3  |  5  |
|-----|-----|-----|
|  A  |     |     |
|     |  A  |     |
|     |     |  A  |

The first row has the note A under the R (root) column. You now know that you must spell the A major chord since you are given the root. The 3rd of A major is C# and the 5th is E. Write the chord tones in the empty space.

|   R   |   3   |   5   |
|-------|-------|-------|
|   A   |  C♯   |   E   |
|       |   A   |       |
|       |       |   A   |

The second row has the note A in the column under the 3rd of a major chord. So, you can either figure out the other chord tones by using the interval distance formulas on each page before every puzzle, or on page 33 if that helps. It's usually easiest to figure out what the root is first and then the rest should comes naturally. A is the 3rd of F major. Now that you know that, just figure out the 5th. C is the 5th of F major.

|   R   |   3   |   5   |
|-------|-------|-------|
|   A   |  C♯   |   E   |
|   F   |   A   |   C   |
|       |       |   A   |

The last row to solve has A set as the 5th of the chord. A is the 5th of D major. Now figure out the 3rd. The 3rd is F# (four half steps from the root). So, the finished puzzle will look like this:

|   R   |   3   |   5   |
|-------|-------|-------|
|   A   |  C♯   |   E   |
|   F   |   A   |   C   |
|   D   |  F♯   |   A   |

Each triad puzzle will have three chords to solve. Each four-note puzzle will have four to solve and so on when there are added notes. If you're a bit confused on how the answers came about, make sure you read all of the parts to "The Foundation" prior to this and do all of the exercises.

Each chord type has a puzzle similar to this one.

*[There is an answer key on my website if you would like to check your answers. The link is at www.JaredCattoor.com. Click on the button that says "Music Theory Puzzles Book." Then click tab called "srewsna" in the drop down menu.]*

That should do it! It's time for you to get started on the puzzles. It's recommended to do one full page every day, until you complete all of the puzzles in this book. If one page is easy, then do more! Just do whatever you're comfortable with.

### How I recommend working with these puzzles.

• Do one full page mentally without using an instrument;

• Then check each row by singing and playing (simultaneously) exactly what you wrote in the box using an instrument;

• If it doesn't sound like the chord type you are working with then you know you made a mistake. Correct it.

I recommend it this way for a few reasons. After doing these puzzles mentally for a while you will just know this information like common sense. Checking them with your instrument will help you know where the notes are on your instrument extremely well and you will train your ear to the sounds. Singing and playing the notes simultaneously will connect your brains understanding of where that sound is on your instrument and it will train your ear to the sounds as well. So over all you will know the information, know how to play it, know what it sounds like and know where to find it on your instrument. That's amazing if you ask me. You can create endless practices with these puzzles as well. That part is up to you, but follow my method and I promise you, you will be a transformed musician.


Thank you so much for working with this book. Congratulations on your willingness to grow!

# Major Triad

## Chord Formula = 1 3 5
### (Also = R M3 P5)

## Interval Method

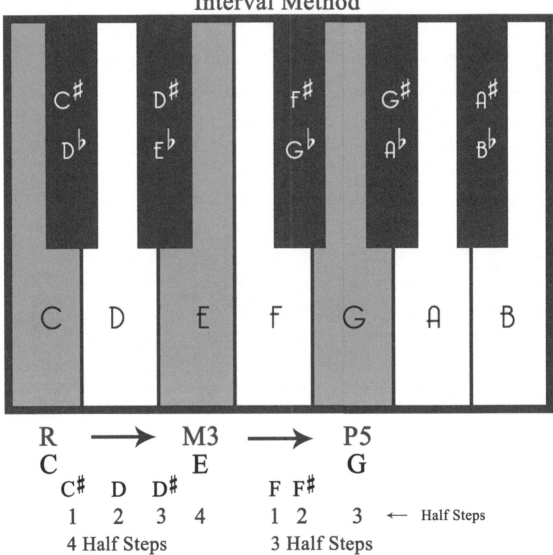

# Major Triads

| R | 3 | 5 |
|---|---|---|
| A |   |   |
|   | A |   |
|   |   | A |

| R | 3 | 5 |
|---|---|---|
| B |   |   |
|   | B |   |
|   |   | B |

| R | 3 | 5 |
|---|---|---|
| C |   |   |
|   | C |   |
|   |   | C |

| R | 3 | 5 |
|---|---|---|
| D |   |   |
|   | D |   |
|   |   | D |

| R | 3 | 5 |
|---|---|---|
| E |   |   |
|   | E |   |
|   |   | E |

| R | 3 | 5 |
|---|---|---|
| F |   |   |
|   | F |   |
|   |   | F |

| R | 3 | 5 |
|---|---|---|
| G |   |   |
|   | G |   |
|   |   | G |

| R | 3 | 5 |
|---|---|---|
| A♭ |   |   |
|   | A♭ |   |
|   |   | A♭ |

| R | 3 | 5 |
|---|---|---|
| B♭ |   |   |
|   | B♭ |   |
|   |   | B♭ |

| R | 3 | 5 |
|---|---|---|
| D♭ |   |   |
|   | D♭ |   |
|   |   | D♭ |

| R | 3 | 5 |
|---|---|---|
| E♭ |   |   |
|   | E♭ |   |
|   |   | E♭ |

| R | 3 | 5 |
|---|---|---|
| F# |   |   |
|   | F# |   |
|   |   | F# |

| R | 3 | 5 |
|---|---|---|
| G# |   |   |
|   | G# |   |
|   |   | G# |

| R | 3 | 5 |
|---|---|---|
| C# |   |   |
|   | C# |   |
|   |   | C# |

| R | 3 | 5 |
|---|---|---|
| D# |   |   |
|   | D# |   |
|   |   | D# |

# Minor Triad

Chord Formula = 1 $^\flat$3 5
(Also = R m3 P5)

## Interval Method

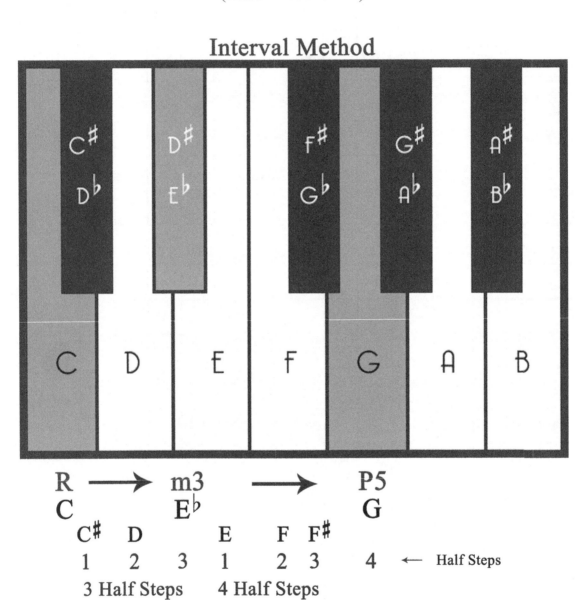

# Minor Triads

| R | ♭3 | 5 |
|---|---|---|
| A | | |
| | A | |
| | | A |

| R | ♭3 | 5 |
|---|---|---|
| B | | |
| | B | |
| | | B |

| R | ♭3 | 5 |
|---|---|---|
| C | | |
| | C | |
| | | C |

| R | ♭3 | 5 |
|---|---|---|
| D | | |
| | D | |
| | | D |

| R | ♭3 | 5 |
|---|---|---|
| E | | |
| | E | |
| | | E |

| R | ♭3 | 5 |
|---|---|---|
| F | | |
| | F | |
| | | F |

| R | ♭3 | 5 |
|---|---|---|
| G | | |
| | G | |
| | | G |

| R | ♭3 | 5 |
|---|---|---|
| C♯ | | |
| | C♯ | |
| | | C♯ |

| R | ♭3 | 5 |
|---|---|---|
| D♯ | | |
| | D♯ | |
| | | D♯ |

| R | ♭3 | 5 |
|---|---|---|
| G♯ | | |
| | G♯ | |
| | | G♯ |

| R | ♭3 | 5 |
|---|---|---|
| F♯ | | |
| | F♯ | |
| | | F♯ |

| R | ♭3 | 5 |
|---|---|---|
| A♭ | | |
| | A♭ | |
| | | A♭ |

| R | ♭3 | 5 |
|---|---|---|
| B♭ | | |
| | B♭ | |
| | | B♭ |

| R | ♭3 | 5 |
|---|---|---|
| E♭ | | |
| | E♭ | |
| | | E♭ |

| R | ♭3 | 5 |
|---|---|---|
| D♭ | | |
| | D♭ | |
| | | D♭ |

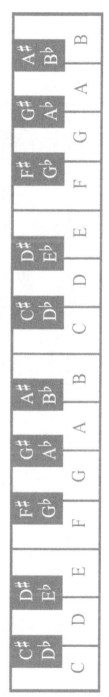

# Diminished Triad

Chord Formula = 1 ♭3 ♭5
(Also = R m3 d5)

## Interval Method

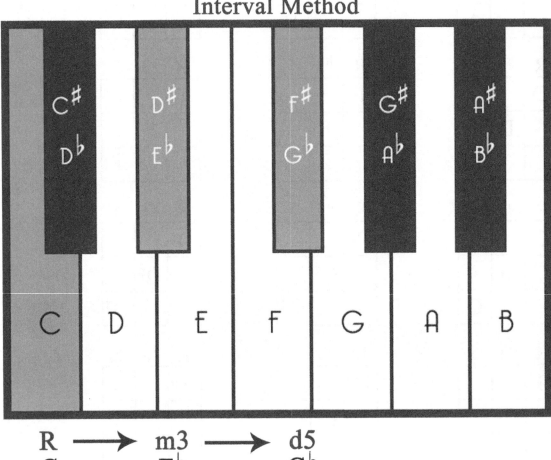

R ⟶ m3 ⟶ d5
C          E♭          G♭

C# D        E    F
1   2   3   1   2   3   ← Half Steps

3 Half Steps     3 Half Steps

# Diminished Triads

| R | ♭3 | ♭5 |
|---|----|----|
| A |   |   |
|   | A |   |
|   |   | A |

| R | ♭3 | ♭5 |
|---|----|----|
| B |   |   |
|   | B |   |
|   |   | B |

| R | ♭3 | ♭5 |
|---|----|----|
| C |   |   |
|   | C |   |
|   |   | C |

| R | ♭3 | ♭5 |
|---|----|----|
| D |   |   |
|   | D |   |
|   |   | D |

| R | ♭3 | ♭5 |
|---|----|----|
| E |   |   |
|   | E |   |
|   |   | E |

| R | ♭3 | ♭5 |
|---|----|----|
| F |   |   |
|   | F |   |
|   |   | F |

| R | ♭3 | ♭5 |
|---|----|----|
| G |   |   |
|   | G |   |
|   |   | G |

| R | ♭3 | ♭5 |
|---|----|----|
| C♯ |   |   |
|   | C♯ |   |
|   |   | C♯ |

| R | ♭3 | ♭5 |
|---|----|----|
| D♯ |   |   |
|   | D♯ |   |
|   |   | D♯ |

| R | ♭3 | ♭5 |
|---|----|----|
| G♯ |   |   |
|   | G♯ |   |
|   |   | G♯ |

| R | ♭3 | ♭5 |
|---|----|----|
| F♯ |   |   |
|   | F♯ |   |
|   |   | F♯ |

| R | ♭3 | ♭5 |
|---|----|----|
| A♭ |   |   |
|   | A♭ |   |
|   |   | A♭ |

| R | ♭3 | ♭5 |
|---|----|----|
| B♭ |   |   |
|   | B♭ |   |
|   |   | B♭ |

| R | ♭3 | ♭5 |
|---|----|----|
| E♭ |   |   |
|   | E♭ |   |
|   |   | E♭ |

| R | ♭3 | ♭5 |
|---|----|----|
| D♭ |   |   |
|   | D♭ |   |
|   |   | D♭ |

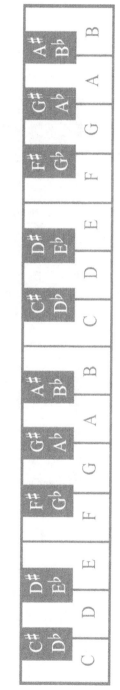

# Augmented Triad

Chord Formula = 1 3 #5
(Also = R M3 A5)

## Interval Method

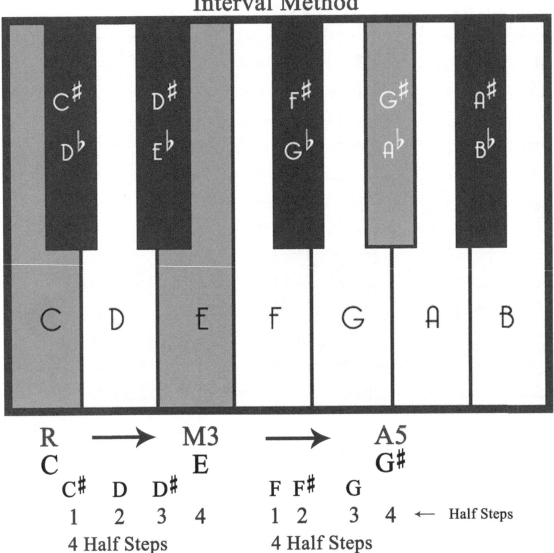

# Augmented Triads

| R | 3 | #5 |
|---|---|---|
| A |   |   |
|   | A |   |
|   |   | A |

| R | 3 | #5 |
|---|---|---|
| B |   |   |
|   | B |   |
|   |   | B |

| R | 3 | #5 |
|---|---|---|
| C |   |   |
|   | C |   |
|   |   | C |

| R | 3 | #5 |
|---|---|---|
| D |   |   |
|   | D |   |
|   |   | D |

| R | 3 | #5 |
|---|---|---|
| E |   |   |
|   | E |   |
|   |   | E |

| R | 3 | #5 |
|---|---|---|
| F |   |   |
|   | F |   |
|   |   | F |

| R | 3 | #5 |
|---|---|---|
| G |   |   |
|   | G |   |
|   |   | G |

| R | 3 | #5 |
|---|---|---|
| C# |   |   |
|   | C# |   |
|   |   | C# |

| R | 3 | #5 |
|---|---|---|
| D# |   |   |
|   | D# |   |
|   |   | D# |

| R | 3 | #5 |
|---|---|---|
| G# |   |   |
|   | G# |   |
|   |   | G# |

| R | 3 | #5 |
|---|---|---|
| F# |   |   |
|   | F# |   |
|   |   | F# |

| R | 3 | #5 |
|---|---|---|
| A♭ |   |   |
|   | A♭ |   |
|   |   | A♭ |

| R | 3 | #5 |
|---|---|---|
| B♭ |   |   |
|   | B♭ |   |
|   |   | B♭ |

| R | 3 | #5 |
|---|---|---|
| E♭ |   |   |
|   | E♭ |   |
|   |   | E♭ |

| R | 3 | #5 |
|---|---|---|
| D♭ |   |   |
|   | D♭ |   |
|   |   | D♭ |

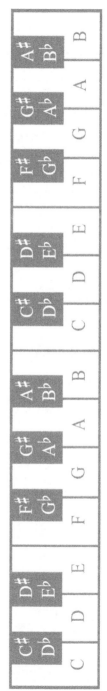

# The Un-organized puzzles!
## (Inversions)

These puzzles are meant to really test your understanding of chord construction. They are dis-organized on purpose to create more of a challenge for you! "Wow that's fun", you might be saying with extreme excitement and pure joy! I totally agree with you! This is fun.

This section of "un-organized puzzles has the Major, Minor, Augmented and Diminished triads in it. Here's an example of what they look like:

| R | 5 | 3 |
|---|---|---|
| F |   |   |
|   | F |   |
|   |   | F |

| R | ♭3 | 5 |
|---|----|---|
| G♭ |   |   |
|   | G♭ |   |
|   |   | G♭ |

| ♯5 | R | 3 |
|----|---|---|
| D♭ |   |   |
|   | D♭ |   |
|   |   | D♭ |

Above we have a Major triad on our left, Minor in the middle and Augmented on the right. Diminished will also be included in the next few pages. When doing these puzzles just pay close attention to the "chord tones" above each puzzle box. These chord types are mixed up without any obvious notification other than the numbers above the boxes. The chord tones define the chord type.

You are still filling in the empty spaces according to the chord tones above the given space. The only difference between these puzzles is that the chord tones are in random places, which can make these puzzles a bit more challenging. The goal after going through this book is to be able to construct any chord type from any chord tone with little or no hesitation. The un-organized sections help tremendously with that.

There will be an "on-organized" section including each type of chord that have in this book.

# Un-Organized Triads
## (Major, Minor, Diminished and Augmented)

| R | 3 | 5 |
|---|---|---|
| C |   |   |
|   | C |   |
|   |   | C |

| R | 5 | 3 |
|---|---|---|
| F |   |   |
|   | F |   |
|   |   | F |

| 3 | 5 | R |
|---|---|---|
| B♭ |   |   |
|   | B♭ |   |
|   |   | B♭ |

| 3 | R | 5 |
|---|---|---|
| E♭ |   |   |
|   | E♭ |   |
|   |   | E♭ |

| 5 | 3 | R |
|---|---|---|
| A♭ |   |   |
|   | A♭ |   |
|   |   | A♭ |

| 5 | R | 3 |
|---|---|---|
| D♭ |   |   |
|   | D♭ |   |
|   |   | D♭ |

| R | ♭3 | 5 |
|---|---|---|
| G♭ |   |   |
|   | G♭ |   |
|   |   | G♭ |

| R | 5 | ♭3 |
|---|---|---|
| C♭ |   |   |
|   | C♭ |   |
|   |   | C♭ |

| ♭3 | 5 | R |
|---|---|---|
| G |   |   |
|   | G |   |
|   |   | G |

| ♭3 | R | 5 |
|---|---|---|
| D |   |   |
|   | D |   |
|   |   | D |

| 5 | ♭3 | R |
|---|---|---|
| A |   |   |
|   | A |   |
|   |   | A |

| 5 | R | ♭3 |
|---|---|---|
| E |   |   |
|   | E |   |
|   |   | E |

| R | ♭3 | ♭5 |
|---|---|---|
| B |   |   |
|   | B |   |
|   |   | B |

| R | ♭5 | ♭3 |
|---|---|---|
| F♯ |   |   |
|   | F♯ |   |
|   |   | F♯ |

| ♭3 | ♭5 | R |
|---|---|---|
| C♯ |   |   |
|   | C♯ |   |
|   |   | C♯ |

Fretboard reference (top to bottom):
A♯/B♭ · B · G♯/A♭ · A · G · F♯/G♭ · F · E · D♯/E♭ · D · C♯/D♭ · C · A♯/B♭ · B · A · G♯/A♭ · G · F♯/G♭ · F · E · D♯/E♭ · D · C♯/D♭ · C

# Un-Organized Triads
## (Major, Minor, Diminished and Augmented)

| R | ♭3 | 5 |
|---|---|---|
| C | | |
| | C | |
| | | C |

| R | 5 | ♭3 |
|---|---|---|
| F | | |
| | F | |
| | | F |

| ♭3 | 5 | R |
|---|---|---|
| B♭ | | |
| | B♭ | |
| | | B♭ |

| ♭3 | R | ♭5 |
|---|---|---|
| E♭ | | |
| | E♭ | |
| | | E♭ |

| ♭5 | ♭3 | R |
|---|---|---|
| A♭ | | |
| | A♭ | |
| | | A♭ |

| ♭5 | R | ♭3 |
|---|---|---|
| D♭ | | |
| | D♭ | |
| | | D♭ |

| R | 3 | ♯5 |
|---|---|---|
| G♭ | | |
| | G♭ | |
| | | G♭ |

| R | ♯5 | 3 |
|---|---|---|
| C♭ | | |
| | C♭ | |
| | | C♭ |

| 3 | ♯5 | R |
|---|---|---|
| G | | |
| | G | |
| | | G |

| 3 | R | 5 |
|---|---|---|
| D | | |
| | D | |
| | | D |

| 5 | 3 | R |
|---|---|---|
| A | | |
| | A | |
| | | A |

| 5 | R | 3 |
|---|---|---|
| E | | |
| | E | |
| | | E |

| R | ♭3 | 5 |
|---|---|---|
| B | | |
| | B | |
| | | B |

| R | ♭5 | ♭3 |
|---|---|---|
| F♯ | | |
| | F♯ | |
| | | F♯ |

| 3 | ♯5 | R |
|---|---|---|
| C♯ | | |
| | C♯ | |
| | | C♯ |

# Sus 4 Chord

Chord Formula = 1 4 5
(Also = R P4 P5)

## Interval Method

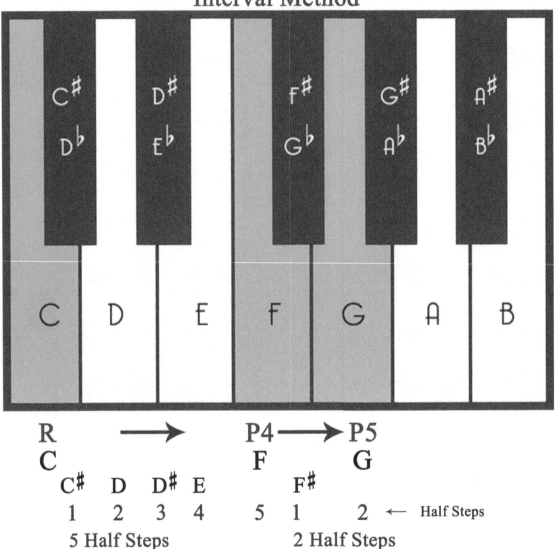

R → P4 → P5
C       F    G

C# D D# E    F#
1   2   3   4     5   1     2 ← Half Steps

5 Half Steps      2 Half Steps

# Sus 4 Chords

| R | 4 | 5 |
|---|---|---|
| A |   |   |
|   | A |   |
|   |   | A |

| R | 4 | 5 |
|---|---|---|
| B |   |   |
|   | B |   |
|   |   | B |

| R | 4 | 5 |
|---|---|---|
| C |   |   |
|   | C |   |
|   |   | C |

| R | 4 | 5 |
|---|---|---|
| D |   |   |
|   | D |   |
|   |   | D |

| R | 4 | 5 |
|---|---|---|
| E |   |   |
|   | E |   |
|   |   | E |

| R | 4 | 5 |
|---|---|---|
| F |   |   |
|   | F |   |
|   |   | F |

| R | 4 | 5 |
|---|---|---|
| G |   |   |
|   | G |   |
|   |   | G |

| R | 4 | 5 |
|---|---|---|
| B♭ |   |   |
|   | B♭ |   |
|   |   | B♭ |

| R | 4 | 5 |
|---|---|---|
| E♭ |   |   |
|   | E♭ |   |
|   |   | E♭ |

| R | 4 | 5 |
|---|---|---|
| A♭ |   |   |
|   | A♭ |   |
|   |   | A♭ |

| R | 4 | 5 |
|---|---|---|
| D♭ |   |   |
|   | D♭ |   |
|   |   | D♭ |

| R | 4 | 5 |
|---|---|---|
| C♯ |   |   |
|   | C♯ |   |
|   |   | C♯ |

| R | 4 | 5 |
|---|---|---|
| F♯ |   |   |
|   | F♯ |   |
|   |   | F♯ |

| R | 4 | 5 |
|---|---|---|
| D♯ |   |   |
|   | D♯ |   |
|   |   | D♯ |

| R | 4 | 5 |
|---|---|---|
| G♯ |   |   |
|   | G♯ |   |
|   |   | G♯ |

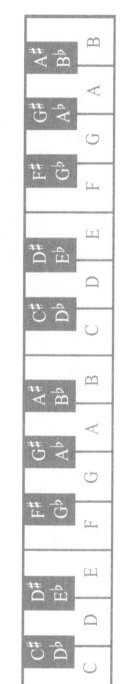

# Sus 2 Chord

## Chord Formula = 1 2 5
(Also = R M2 P5)

## Interval Method

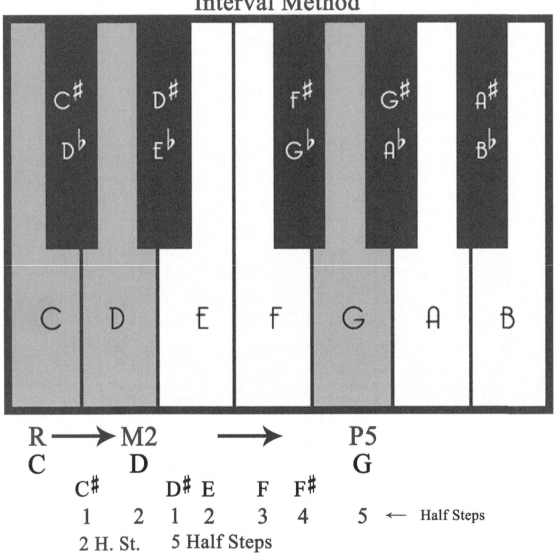

R → M2 → P5
C    D     G

C♯  D♯ E  F  F♯
1    2  1  2  3  4  5  ← Half Steps
2 H. St.   5 Half Steps

# Sus 2 Chords

| R | 2 | 5 |
|---|---|---|
| A |   |   |
|   | A |   |
|   |   | A |

| R | 2 | 5 |
|---|---|---|
| B |   |   |
|   | B |   |
|   |   | B |

| R | 2 | 5 |
|---|---|---|
| C |   |   |
|   | C |   |
|   |   | C |

| R | 2 | 5 |
|---|---|---|
| D |   |   |
|   | D |   |
|   |   | D |

| R | 2 | 5 |
|---|---|---|
| E |   |   |
|   | E |   |
|   |   | E |

| R | 2 | 5 |
|---|---|---|
| F |   |   |
|   | F |   |
|   |   | F |

| R | 2 | 5 |
|---|---|---|
| G |   |   |
|   | G |   |
|   |   | G |

| R | 2 | 5 |
|---|---|---|
| B♭ |   |   |
|   | B♭ |   |
|   |   | B♭ |

| R | 2 | 5 |
|---|---|---|
| E♭ |   |   |
|   | E♭ |   |
|   |   | E♭ |

| R | 2 | 5 |
|---|---|---|
| A♭ |   |   |
|   | A♭ |   |
|   |   | A♭ |

| R | 2 | 5 |
|---|---|---|
| D♭ |   |   |
|   | D♭ |   |
|   |   | D♭ |

| R | 2 | 5 |
|---|---|---|
| C# |   |   |
|   | C# |   |
|   |   | C# |

| R | 2 | 5 |
|---|---|---|
| F# |   |   |
|   | F# |   |
|   |   | F# |

| R | 2 | 5 |
|---|---|---|
| D# |   |   |
|   | D# |   |
|   |   | D# |

| R | 2 | 5 |
|---|---|---|
| G# |   |   |
|   | G# |   |
|   |   | G# |

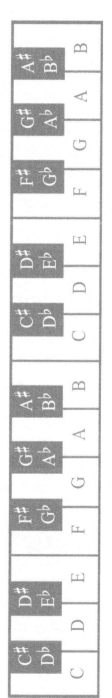

# Un-Organized Sus Chords

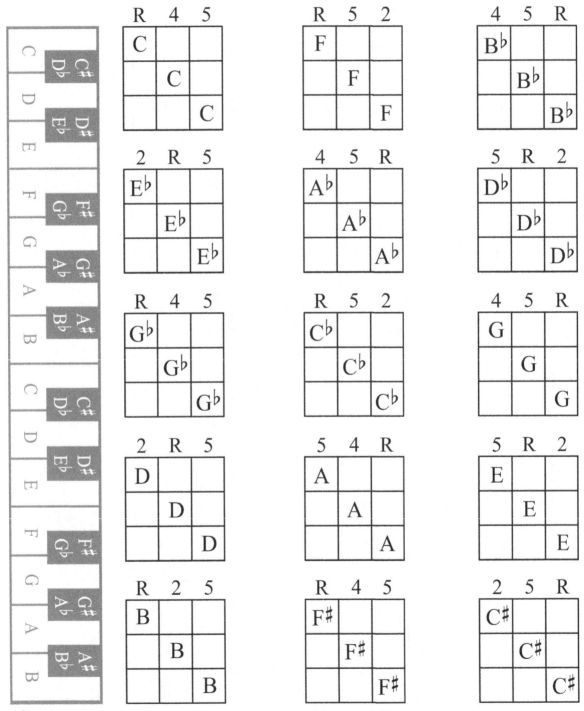

Part III
# FOUR NOTE CHORD PUZZLES

# Major Add 2 Chord

## Chord Formula = 1 2 3 5
### (Also = R M2 M3 P5)

## Interval Method

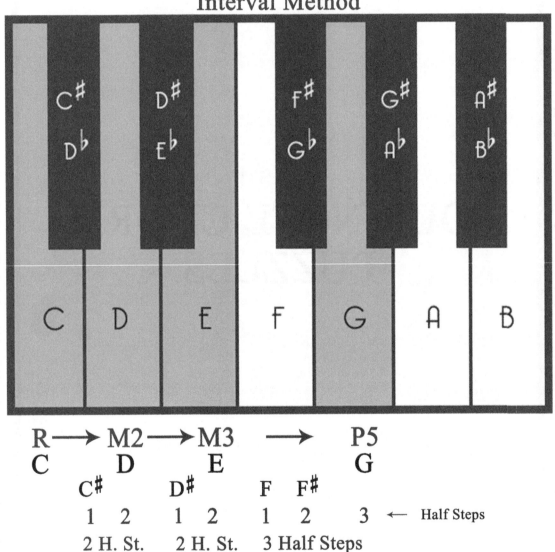

| | | | | |
|---|---|---|---|---|
| R → | M2 → | M3 | → | P5 |
| C | D | E | | G |
| C# | D# | F | F# | |
| 1  2 | 1  2 | 1  2 | 3 | ← Half Steps |
| 2 H. St. | 2 H. St. | 3 Half Steps | | |

# Major Add 2 Chord

| R | 2 | 3 | 5 |
|---|---|---|---|
| C | | | |
| | C | | |
| | | C | |
| | | | C |

| R | 2 | 3 | 5 |
|---|---|---|---|
| G | | | |
| | G | | |
| | | G | |
| | | | G |

| R | 2 | 3 | 5 |
|---|---|---|---|
| D | | | |
| | D | | |
| | | D | |
| | | | D |

| R | 2 | 3 | 5 |
|---|---|---|---|
| A | | | |
| | A | | |
| | | A | |
| | | | A |

| R | 2 | 3 | 5 |
|---|---|---|---|
| E | | | |
| | E | | |
| | | E | |
| | | | E |

| R | 2 | 3 | 5 |
|---|---|---|---|
| B | | | |
| | B | | |
| | | B | |
| | | | B |

| R | 2 | 3 | 5 |
|---|---|---|---|
| F# | | | |
| | F# | | |
| | | F# | |
| | | | F# |

| R | 2 | 3 | 5 |
|---|---|---|---|
| F | | | |
| | F | | |
| | | F | |
| | | | F |

| R | 2 | 3 | 5 |
|---|---|---|---|
| B♭ | | | |
| | B♭ | | |
| | | B♭ | |
| | | | B♭ |

| R | 2 | 3 | 5 |
|---|---|---|---|
| E♭ | | | |
| | E♭ | | |
| | | E♭ | |
| | | | E♭ |

| R | 2 | 3 | 5 |
|---|---|---|---|
| A♭ | | | |
| | A♭ | | |
| | | A♭ | |
| | | | A♭ |

| R | 2 | 3 | 5 |
|---|---|---|---|
| D♭ | | | |
| | D♭ | | |
| | | D♭ | |
| | | | D♭ |

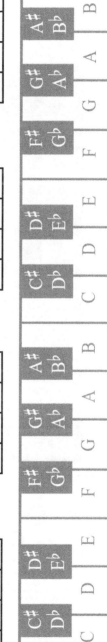

# Major 6<sup>th</sup> Chord

## Chord Formula = 1 3 5 6
### (Also = R M3 P5 M6)

## Interval Method

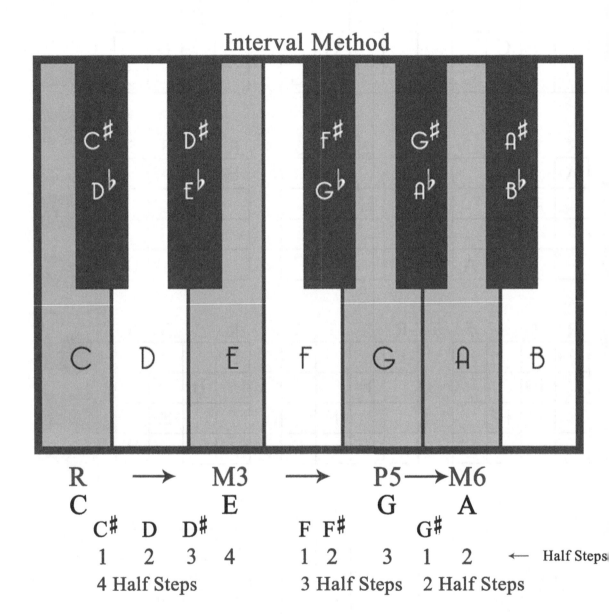

# Major 6th Chord

| R | 3 | 5 | 6 |
|---|---|---|---|
| C |   |   |   |
|   | C |   |   |
|   |   | C |   |
|   |   |   | C |

| R | 3 | 5 | 6 |
|---|---|---|---|
| G |   |   |   |
|   | G |   |   |
|   |   | G |   |
|   |   |   | G |

| R | 3 | 5 | 6 |
|---|---|---|---|
| D |   |   |   |
|   | D |   |   |
|   |   | D |   |
|   |   |   | D |

| R | 3 | 5 | 6 |
|---|---|---|---|
| A |   |   |   |
|   | A |   |   |
|   |   | A |   |
|   |   |   | A |

| R | 3 | 5 | 6 |
|---|---|---|---|
| E |   |   |   |
|   | E |   |   |
|   |   | E |   |
|   |   |   | E |

| R | 3 | 5 | 6 |
|---|---|---|---|
| B |   |   |   |
|   | B |   |   |
|   |   | B |   |
|   |   |   | B |

| R | 3 | 5 | 6 |
|---|---|---|---|
| F♯ |   |   |   |
|   | F♯ |   |   |
|   |   | F♯ |   |
|   |   |   | F♯ |

| R | 3 | 5 | 6 |
|---|---|---|---|
| F |   |   |   |
|   | F |   |   |
|   |   | F |   |
|   |   |   | F |

| R | 3 | 5 | 6 |
|---|---|---|---|
| B♭ |   |   |   |
|   | B♭ |   |   |
|   |   | B♭ |   |
|   |   |   | B♭ |

| R | 3 | 5 | 6 |
|---|---|---|---|
| E♭ |   |   |   |
|   | E♭ |   |   |
|   |   | E♭ |   |
|   |   |   | E♭ |

| R | 3 | 5 | 6 |
|---|---|---|---|
| A♭ |   |   |   |
|   | A♭ |   |   |
|   |   | A♭ |   |
|   |   |   | A♭ |

| R | 3 | 5 | 6 |
|---|---|---|---|
| D♭ |   |   |   |
|   | D♭ |   |   |
|   |   | D♭ |   |
|   |   |   | D♭ |

63

# Major 7th Chord

## Chord Formula = 1 3 5 7
### (Also = R M3 P5 M7)

## Interval Method

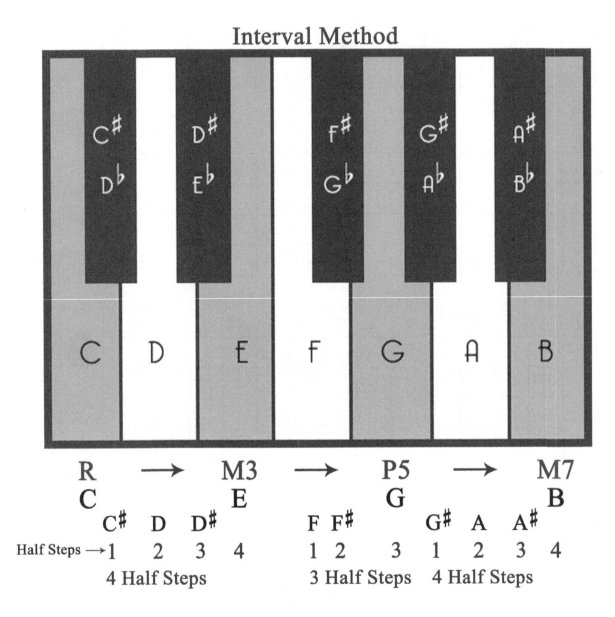

| R | → | M3 | → | P5 | → | M7 |
|---|---|----|---|----|---|----|
| C | | E | | G | | B |

| | C# | D | D# | | F | F# | | G# | A | A# | |
|---|----|---|----|---|---|----|---|----|---|----|---|

Half Steps → 1   2   3   4    1   2   3    1   2   3   4

4 Half Steps     3 Half Steps   4 Half Steps

# Major 7<sup>th</sup> Chord

| R | 3 | 5 | 7 |
|---|---|---|---|
| A |   |   |   |
|   | A |   |   |
|   |   | A |   |
|   |   |   | A |

| R | 3 | 5 | 7 |
|---|---|---|---|
| B |   |   |   |
|   | B |   |   |
|   |   | B |   |
|   |   |   | B |

| R | 3 | 5 | 7 |
|---|---|---|---|
| C |   |   |   |
|   | C |   |   |
|   |   | C |   |
|   |   |   | C |

| R | 3 | 5 | 7 |
|---|---|---|---|
| D |   |   |   |
|   | D |   |   |
|   |   | D |   |
|   |   |   | D |

| R | 3 | 5 | 7 |
|---|---|---|---|
| E |   |   |   |
|   | E |   |   |
|   |   | E |   |
|   |   |   | E |

| R | 3 | 5 | 7 |
|---|---|---|---|
| F |   |   |   |
|   | F |   |   |
|   |   | F |   |
|   |   |   | F |

| R | 3 | 5 | 7 |
|---|---|---|---|
| G |   |   |   |
|   | G |   |   |
|   |   | G |   |
|   |   |   | G |

| R | 3 | 5 | 7 |
|---|---|---|---|
| F# |   |   |   |
|   | F# |   |   |
|   |   | F# |   |
|   |   |   | F# |

| R | 3 | 5 | 7 |
|---|---|---|---|
| C# |   |   |   |
|   | C# |   |   |
|   |   | C# |   |
|   |   |   | C# |

| R | 3 | 5 | 7 |
|---|---|---|---|
| E♭ |   |   |   |
|   | E♭ |   |   |
|   |   | E♭ |   |
|   |   |   | E♭ |

| R | 3 | 5 | 7 |
|---|---|---|---|
| A♭ |   |   |   |
|   | A♭ |   |   |
|   |   | A♭ |   |
|   |   |   | A♭ |

| R | 3 | 5 | 7 |
|---|---|---|---|
| B♭ |   |   |   |
|   | B♭ |   |   |
|   |   | B♭ |   |
|   |   |   | B♭ |

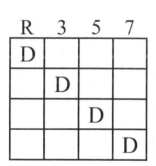

# Dominant 7th Chord

Chord Formula = 1 3 5 ♭7
(Also = R M3 P5 m7)

## Interval Method

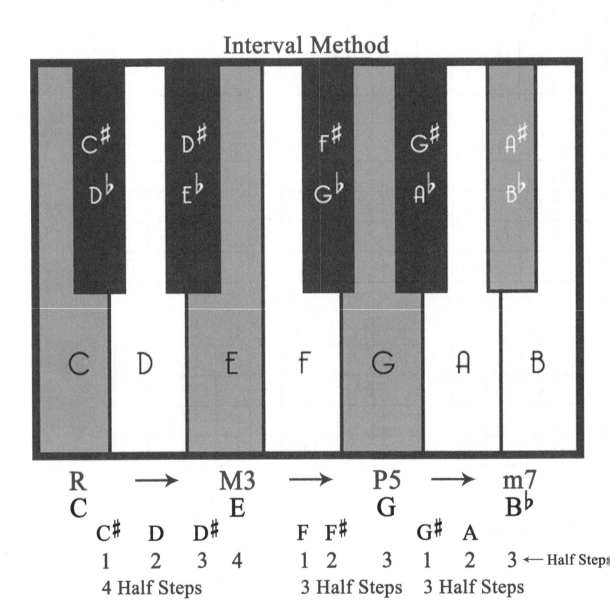

R   →   M3   →   P5   →   m7
C          E          G          B♭

C#   D   D#       F   F#      G#   A
1    2    3    4      1    2     3    1    2    3 ← Half Step
4 Half Steps       3 Half Steps   3 Half Steps

# Dominant 7th Chord

| R | 3 | 5 | ♭7 |
|---|---|---|---|
| A | | | |
| | A | | |
| | | A | |
| | | | A |

| R | 3 | 5 | ♭7 |
|---|---|---|---|
| B | | | |
| | B | | |
| | | B | |
| | | | B |

| R | 3 | 5 | ♭7 |
|---|---|---|---|
| C | | | |
| | C | | |
| | | C | |
| | | | C |

| R | 3 | 5 | ♭7 |
|---|---|---|---|
| D | | | |
| | D | | |
| | | D | |
| | | | D |

| R | 3 | 5 | ♭7 |
|---|---|---|---|
| E | | | |
| | E | | |
| | | E | |
| | | | E |

| R | 3 | 5 | ♭7 |
|---|---|---|---|
| F | | | |
| | F | | |
| | | F | |
| | | | F |

| R | 3 | 5 | ♭7 |
|---|---|---|---|
| G | | | |
| | G | | |
| | | G | |
| | | | G |

| R | 3 | 5 | ♭7 |
|---|---|---|---|
| F♯ | | | |
| | F♯ | | |
| | | F♯ | |
| | | | F♯ |

| R | 3 | 5 | ♭7 |
|---|---|---|---|
| C♯ | | | |
| | C♯ | | |
| | | C♯ | |
| | | | C♯ |

| R | 3 | 5 | ♭7 |
|---|---|---|---|
| B♭ | | | |
| | B♭ | | |
| | | B♭ | |
| | | | B♭ |

| R | 3 | 5 | ♭7 |
|---|---|---|---|
| E♭ | | | |
| | E♭ | | |
| | | E♭ | |
| | | | E♭ |

| R | 3 | 5 | ♭7 |
|---|---|---|---|
| A♭ | | | |
| | A♭ | | |
| | | A♭ | |
| | | | A♭ |

# Dominant 7<sup>th</sup> Sus 4 Chord

Chord Formula = 1 4 5 ♭7
(Also = R P4 P5 m7)

## Interval Method

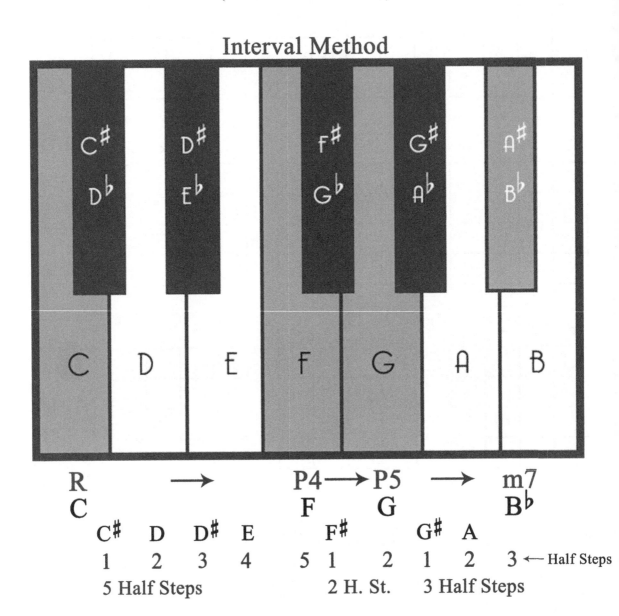

R
C

C#   D   D#   E     F#     G#   A

P4 → P5 → m7
F    G    B♭

1   2   3   4   5   1   2   1   2   3 ← Half Steps

5 Half Steps     2 H. St.    3 Half Steps

# Dominant 7ᵗʰ Sus 4 Chord

| R | 4 | 5 | ♭7 |
|---|---|---|---|
| A |   |   |   |
|   | A |   |   |
|   |   | A |   |
|   |   |   | A |

| R | 4 | 5 | ♭7 |
|---|---|---|---|
| B |   |   |   |
|   | B |   |   |
|   |   | B |   |
|   |   |   | B |

| R | 4 | 5 | ♭7 |
|---|---|---|---|
| C |   |   |   |
|   | C |   |   |
|   |   | C |   |
|   |   |   | C |

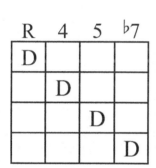

| R | 4 | 5 | ♭7 |
|---|---|---|---|
| D |   |   |   |
|   | D |   |   |
|   |   | D |   |
|   |   |   | D |

| R | 4 | 5 | ♭7 |
|---|---|---|---|
| E |   |   |   |
|   | E |   |   |
|   |   | E |   |
|   |   |   | E |

| R | 4 | 5 | ♭7 |
|---|---|---|---|
| F |   |   |   |
|   | F |   |   |
|   |   | F |   |
|   |   |   | F |

| R | 4 | 5 | ♭7 |
|---|---|---|---|
| G |   |   |   |
|   | G |   |   |
|   |   | G |   |
|   |   |   | G |

| R | 4 | 5 | ♭7 |
|---|---|---|---|
| F# |   |   |   |
|   | F# |   |   |
|   |   | F# |   |
|   |   |   | F# |

| R | 4 | 5 | ♭7 |
|---|---|---|---|
| C# |   |   |   |
|   | C# |   |   |
|   |   | C# |   |
|   |   |   | C# |

| R | 4 | 5 | ♭7 |
|---|---|---|---|
| B♭ |   |   |   |
|   | B♭ |   |   |
|   |   | B♭ |   |
|   |   |   | B♭ |

| R | 4 | 5 | ♭7 |
|---|---|---|---|
| E♭ |   |   |   |
|   | E♭ |   |   |
|   |   | E♭ |   |
|   |   |   | E♭ |

| R | 4 | 5 | ♭7 |
|---|---|---|---|
| A♭ |   |   |   |
|   | A♭ |   |   |
|   |   | A♭ |   |
|   |   |   | A♭ |

# Augmented 7th Chord

(Dominant 7 #5)

## Chord Formula = 1 3 #5 ♭7
(Also = R M3 A5 m7)

## Interval Method

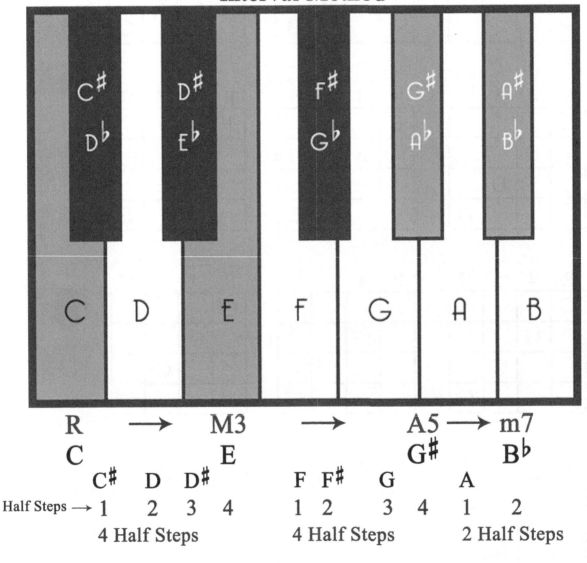

| R | → | M3 | → | A5 | → | m7 |
|---|---|---|---|----|---|----|
| C | | E | | G# | | B♭ |

|  | C# | D | D# |  | F | F# | G |  | A |  |
|--|----|---|----|--|---|----|---|--|---|--|
| Half Steps → | 1 | 2 | 3 | 4 | 1 | 2 | 3 | 4 | 1 | 2 |
|  | 4 Half Steps | | | | 4 Half Steps | | | | 2 Half Steps | |

# Augmented 7th Chord
(Dominant 7 #5)

| R | 3 | #5 | ♭7 |
|---|---|----|----|
| C |   |    |    |
|   | C |    |    |
|   |   | C  |    |
|   |   |    | C  |

| R | 3 | #5 | ♭7 |
|---|---|----|----|
| G |   |    |    |
|   | G |    |    |
|   |   | G  |    |
|   |   |    | G  |

| R | 3 | #5 | ♭7 |
|---|---|----|----|
| D |   |    |    |
|   | D |    |    |
|   |   | D  |    |
|   |   |    | D  |

| R | 3 | #5 | ♭7 |
|---|---|----|----|
| A |   |    |    |
|   | A |    |    |
|   |   | A  |    |
|   |   |    | A  |

| R | 3 | #5 | ♭7 |
|---|---|----|----|
| E |   |    |    |
|   | E |    |    |
|   |   | E  |    |
|   |   |    | E  |

| R | 3 | #5 | ♭7 |
|---|---|----|----|
| B |   |    |    |
|   | B |    |    |
|   |   | B  |    |
|   |   |    | B  |

| R | 3 | #5 | ♭7 |
|----|----|-----|-----|
| F# |    |     |     |
|    | F# |     |     |
|    |    | F#  |     |
|    |    |     | F#  |

| R | 3 | #5 | ♭7 |
|---|---|----|----|
| F |   |    |    |
|   | F |    |    |
|   |   | F  |    |
|   |   |    | F  |

| R | 3 | #5 | ♭7 |
|----|----|-----|-----|
| B♭ |    |     |     |
|    | B♭ |     |     |
|    |    | B♭  |     |
|    |    |     | B♭  |

| R | 3 | #5 | ♭7 |
|----|----|-----|-----|
| E♭ |    |     |     |
|    | E♭ |     |     |
|    |    | E♭  |     |
|    |    |     | E♭  |

| R | 3 | #5 | ♭7 |
|----|----|-----|-----|
| A♭ |    |     |     |
|    | A♭ |     |     |
|    |    | A♭  |     |
|    |    |     | A♭  |

| R | 3 | #5 | ♭7 |
|----|----|-----|-----|
| D♭ |    |     |     |
|    | D♭ |     |     |
|    |    | D♭  |     |
|    |    |     | D♭  |

# Minor Add 2 Chord

Chord Formula = 1 2 $^\flat$3 5
(Also = R M2 m3 P5)

## Interval Method

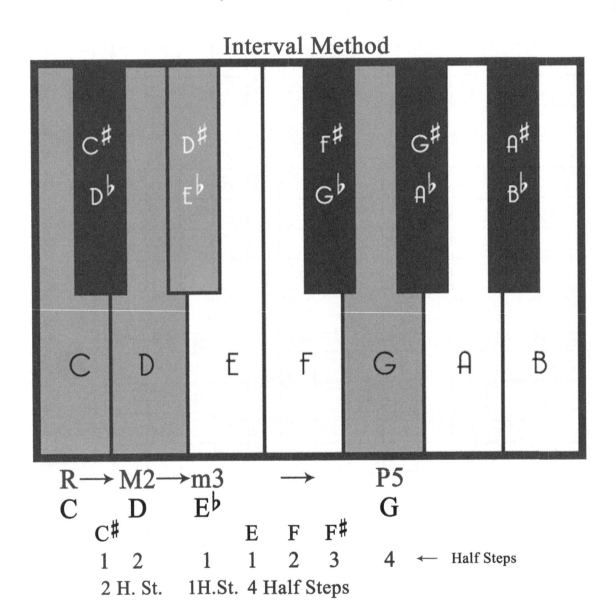

# Minor Add 2 Chord

| R | 2 | ♭3 | 5 |
|---|---|---|---|
| C |   |    |   |
|   | C |    |   |
|   |   | C  |   |
|   |   |    | C |

| R | 2 | ♭3 | 5 |
|---|---|---|---|
| G |   |    |   |
|   | G |    |   |
|   |   | G  |   |
|   |   |    | G |

| R | 2 | ♭3 | 5 |
|---|---|---|---|
| D |   |    |   |
|   | D |    |   |
|   |   | D  |   |
|   |   |    | D |

| R | 2 | ♭3 | 5 |
|---|---|---|---|
| A |   |    |   |
|   | A |    |   |
|   |   | A  |   |
|   |   |    | A |

| R | 2 | ♭3 | 5 |
|---|---|---|---|
| E |   |    |   |
|   | E |    |   |
|   |   | E  |   |
|   |   |    | E |

| R | 2 | ♭3 | 5 |
|---|---|---|---|
| B |   |    |   |
|   | B |    |   |
|   |   | B  |   |
|   |   |    | B |

| R | 2 | ♭3 | 5 |
|---|---|---|---|
| F♯ |   |    |   |
|   | F♯ |    |   |
|   |   | F♯  |   |
|   |   |    | F♯ |

| R | 2 | ♭3 | 5 |
|---|---|---|---|
| F |   |    |   |
|   | F |    |   |
|   |   | F  |   |
|   |   |    | F |

| R | 2 | ♭3 | 5 |
|---|---|---|---|
| B♭ |   |    |   |
|   | B♭ |    |   |
|   |   | B♭  |   |
|   |   |    | B♭ |

| R | 2 | ♭3 | 5 |
|---|---|---|---|
| E♭ |   |    |   |
|   | E♭ |    |   |
|   |   | E♭  |   |
|   |   |    | E♭ |

| R | 2 | ♭3 | 5 |
|---|---|---|---|
| A♭ |   |    |   |
|   | A♭ |    |   |
|   |   | A♭  |   |
|   |   |    | A♭ |

| R | 2 | ♭3 | 5 |
|---|---|---|---|
| D♭ |   |    |   |
|   | D♭ |    |   |
|   |   | D♭  |   |
|   |   |    | D♭ |

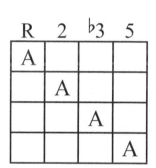

# Minor 6th Chord

Chord Formula = 1 ♭3 5 6
(Also = R m3 P5 M6)

## Interval Method

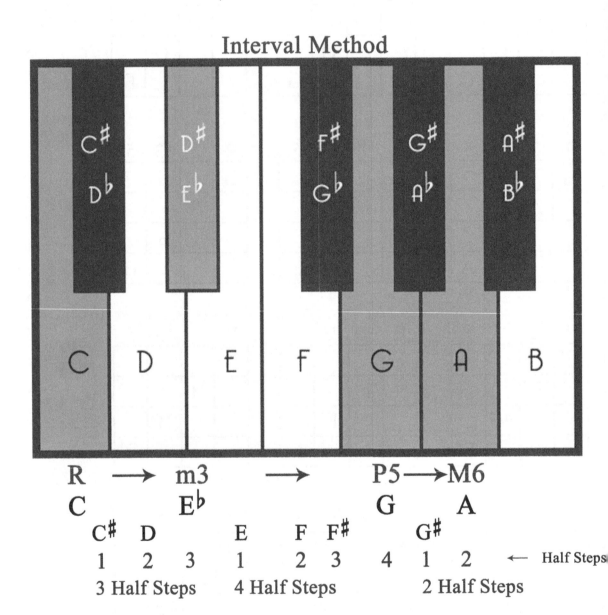

R    →    m3    →    P5 → M6
C          E♭              G     A

  C#  D      E    F  F#     G#

  1   2   3    1   2   3   4   1   2    ← Half Steps

  3 Half Steps      4 Half Steps      2 Half Steps

# Minor 6th Chord

| R | ♭3 | 5 | 6 |
|---|---|---|---|
| C | | | |
| | C | | |
| | | C | |
| | | | C |

| R | ♭3 | 5 | 6 |
|---|---|---|---|
| G | | | |
| | G | | |
| | | G | |
| | | | G |

| R | ♭3 | 5 | 6 |
|---|---|---|---|
| D | | | |
| | D | | |
| | | D | |
| | | | D |

| R | ♭3 | 5 | 6 |
|---|---|---|---|
| A | | | |
| | A | | |
| | | A | |
| | | | A |

| R | ♭3 | 5 | 6 |
|---|---|---|---|
| E | | | |
| | E | | |
| | | E | |
| | | | E |

| R | ♭3 | 5 | 6 |
|---|---|---|---|
| B | | | |
| | B | | |
| | | B | |
| | | | B |

| R | ♭3 | 5 | 6 |
|---|---|---|---|
| F# | | | |
| | F# | | |
| | | F# | |
| | | | F# |

| R | ♭3 | 5 | 6 |
|---|---|---|---|
| F | | | |
| | F | | |
| | | F | |
| | | | F |

| R | ♭3 | 5 | 6 |
|---|---|---|---|
| B♭ | | | |
| | B♭ | | |
| | | B♭ | |
| | | | B♭ |

| R | ♭3 | 5 | 6 |
|---|---|---|---|
| E♭ | | | |
| | E♭ | | |
| | | E♭ | |
| | | | E♭ |

| R | ♭3 | 5 | 6 |
|---|---|---|---|
| A♭ | | | |
| | A♭ | | |
| | | A♭ | |
| | | | A♭ |

| R | ♭3 | 5 | 6 |
|---|---|---|---|
| D♭ | | | |
| | D♭ | | |
| | | D♭ | |
| | | | D♭ |

# Minor 7th Chord

Chord Formula = 1 ♭3 5 ♭7
(Also = R m3 P5 m7)

## Interval Method

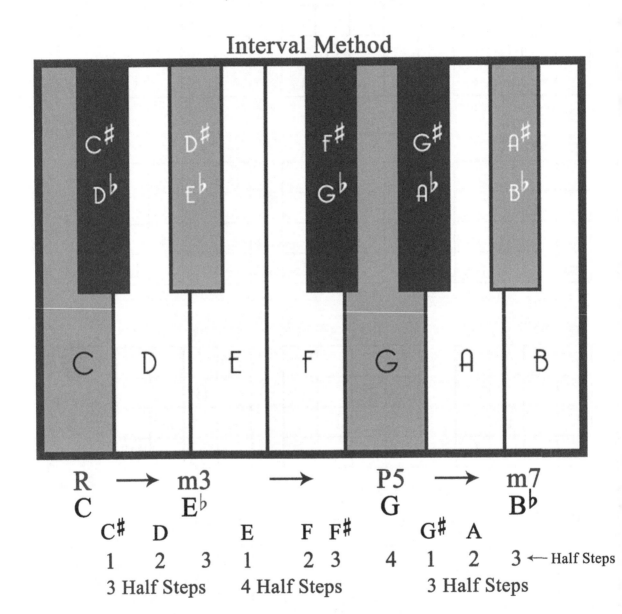

R → m3 → P5 → m7
C    E♭      G    B♭

C# D   E  F F#   G# A

1  2 3 1  2 3   4 1  2   3 ← Half Steps

3 Half Steps   4 Half Steps   3 Half Steps

# Minor 7th Chord

| R | ♭3 | 5 | ♭7 |
|---|---|---|---|
| A | | | |
| | A | | |
| | | A | |
| | | | A |

| R | ♭3 | 5 | ♭7 |
|---|---|---|---|
| B | | | |
| | B | | |
| | | B | |
| | | | B |

| R | ♭3 | 5 | ♭7 |
|---|---|---|---|
| C | | | |
| | C | | |
| | | C | |
| | | | C |

| R | ♭3 | 5 | ♭7 |
|---|---|---|---|
| D | | | |
| | D | | |
| | | D | |
| | | | D |

| R | ♭3 | 5 | ♭7 |
|---|---|---|---|
| E | | | |
| | E | | |
| | | E | |
| | | | E |

| R | ♭3 | 5 | ♭7 |
|---|---|---|---|
| F | | | |
| | F | | |
| | | F | |
| | | | F |

| R | ♭3 | 5 | ♭7 |
|---|---|---|---|
| G | | | |
| | G | | |
| | | G | |
| | | | G |

| R | ♭3 | 5 | ♭7 |
|---|---|---|---|
| F# | | | |
| | F# | | |
| | | F# | |
| | | | F# |

| R | ♭3 | 5 | ♭7 |
|---|---|---|---|
| C# | | | |
| | C# | | |
| | | C# | |
| | | | C# |

| R | ♭3 | 5 | ♭7 |
|---|---|---|---|
| E♭ | | | |
| | E♭ | | |
| | | E♭ | |
| | | | E♭ |

| R | ♭3 | 5 | ♭7 |
|---|---|---|---|
| A♭ | | | |
| | A♭ | | |
| | | A♭ | |
| | | | A♭ |

| R | ♭3 | 5 | ♭7 |
|---|---|---|---|
| B♭ | | | |
| | B♭ | | |
| | | B♭ | |
| | | | B♭ |

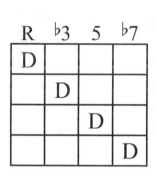

77

# Minor 7th ♭5 Chord

## (Half Diminished)

Chord Formula = 1 ♭3 ♭5 ♭7

(Also = R m3 d5 m7)

## Interval Method

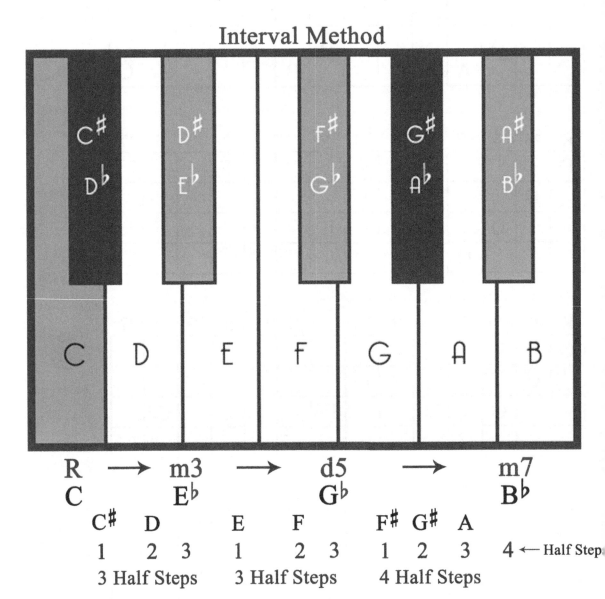

R →　m3 →　d5 →　m7

C　　E♭　　G♭　　B♭

C# D　E F　F# G# A

1　2 3　1　2 3　1　2 3　4 ← Half Step

3 Half Steps　3 Half Steps　4 Half Steps

# Minor 7th ♭5 Chord
## (Half Diminished)

| R | ♭3 | ♭5 | ♭7 |
|---|----|----|----|
| A |   |   |   |
|   | A |   |   |
|   |   | A |   |
|   |   |   | A |

| R | ♭3 | ♭5 | ♭7 |
|---|----|----|----|
| B |   |   |   |
|   | B |   |   |
|   |   | B |   |
|   |   |   | B |

| R | ♭3 | ♭5 | ♭7 |
|---|----|----|----|
| C |   |   |   |
|   | C |   |   |
|   |   | C |   |
|   |   |   | C |

| R | ♭3 | ♭5 | ♭7 |
|---|----|----|----|
| D |   |   |   |
|   | D |   |   |
|   |   | D |   |
|   |   |   | D |

| R | ♭3 | ♭5 | ♭7 |
|---|----|----|----|
| E |   |   |   |
|   | E |   |   |
|   |   | E |   |
|   |   |   | E |

| R | ♭3 | ♭5 | ♭7 |
|---|----|----|----|
| F |   |   |   |
|   | F |   |   |
|   |   | F |   |
|   |   |   | F |

| R | ♭3 | ♭5 | ♭7 |
|---|----|----|----|
| G |   |   |   |
|   | G |   |   |
|   |   | G |   |
|   |   |   | G |

| R | ♭3 | ♭5 | ♭7 |
|---|----|----|----|
| F# |   |   |   |
|   | F# |   |   |
|   |   | F# |   |
|   |   |   | F# |

| R | ♭3 | ♭5 | ♭7 |
|---|----|----|----|
| C# |   |   |   |
|   | C# |   |   |
|   |   | C# |   |
|   |   |   | C# |

| R | ♭3 | ♭5 | ♭7 |
|---|----|----|----|
| E♭ |   |   |   |
|   | E♭ |   |   |
|   |   | E♭ |   |
|   |   |   | E♭ |

| R | ♭3 | ♭5 | ♭7 |
|---|----|----|----|
| A♭ |   |   |   |
|   | A♭ |   |   |
|   |   | A♭ |   |
|   |   |   | A♭ |

| R | ♭3 | ♭5 | ♭7 |
|---|----|----|----|
| B♭ |   |   |   |
|   | B♭ |   |   |
|   |   | B♭ |   |
|   |   |   | B♭ |

# Diminished 7th Chord
## (Fully Diminished)

Chord Formula = 1 ♭3 ♭5 ♭♭7
(Also = R m3 d5 d7)

## Interval Method

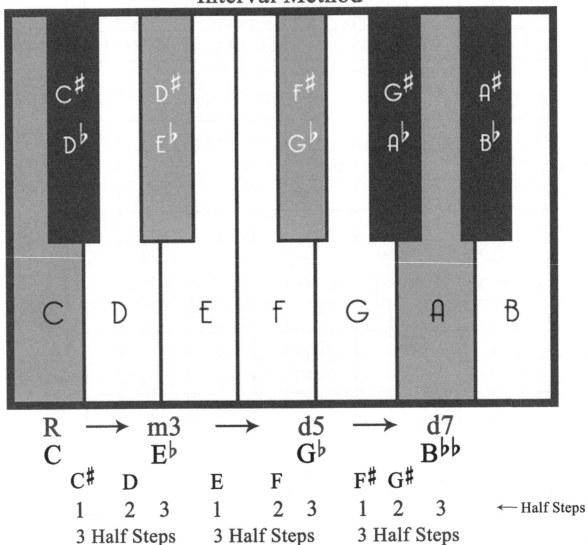

# Diminished 7th Chord
## (Fully Diminished)

| R | ♭3 | ♭5 | ♭♭7 |
|---|----|----|-----|
| A |   |   |   |
|   | A |   |   |
|   |   | A |   |
|   |   |   | A |

| R | ♭3 | ♭5 | ♭♭7 |
|---|----|----|-----|
| B |   |   |   |
|   | B |   |   |
|   |   | B |   |
|   |   |   | B |

| R | ♭3 | ♭5 | ♭♭7 |
|---|----|----|-----|
| C |   |   |   |
|   | C |   |   |
|   |   | C |   |
|   |   |   | C |

| R | ♭3 | ♭5 | ♭♭7 |
|---|----|----|-----|
| D |   |   |   |
|   | D |   |   |
|   |   | D |   |
|   |   |   | D |

| R | ♭3 | ♭5 | ♭♭7 |
|---|----|----|-----|
| E |   |   |   |
|   | E |   |   |
|   |   | E |   |
|   |   |   | E |

| R | ♭3 | ♭5 | ♭♭7 |
|---|----|----|-----|
| F |   |   |   |
|   | F |   |   |
|   |   | F |   |
|   |   |   | F |

| R | ♭3 | ♭5 | ♭♭7 |
|---|----|----|-----|
| G |   |   |   |
|   | G |   |   |
|   |   | G |   |
|   |   |   | G |

| R | ♭3 | ♭5 | ♭♭7 |
|----|----|----|-----|
| F# |   |   |   |
|   | F# |   |   |
|   |   | F# |   |
|   |   |   | F# |

| R | ♭3 | ♭5 | ♭♭7 |
|----|----|----|-----|
| C# |   |   |   |
|   | C# |   |   |
|   |   | C# |   |
|   |   |   | C# |

| R | ♭3 | ♭5 | ♭♭7 |
|----|----|----|-----|
| E♭ |   |   |   |
|   | E♭ |   |   |
|   |   | E♭ |   |
|   |   |   | E♭ |

| R | ♭3 | ♭5 | ♭♭7 |
|----|----|----|-----|
| A♭ |   |   |   |
|   | A♭ |   |   |
|   |   | A♭ |   |
|   |   |   | A♭ |

| R | ♭3 | ♭5 | ♭♭7 |
|----|----|----|-----|
| B♭ |   |   |   |
|   | B♭ |   |   |
|   |   | B♭ |   |
|   |   |   | B♭ |

81

# Minor Major 7<sup>th</sup> Chord

Chord Formula = 1 ♭3 5 7
(Also = R m3 P5 M7)

## Interval Method

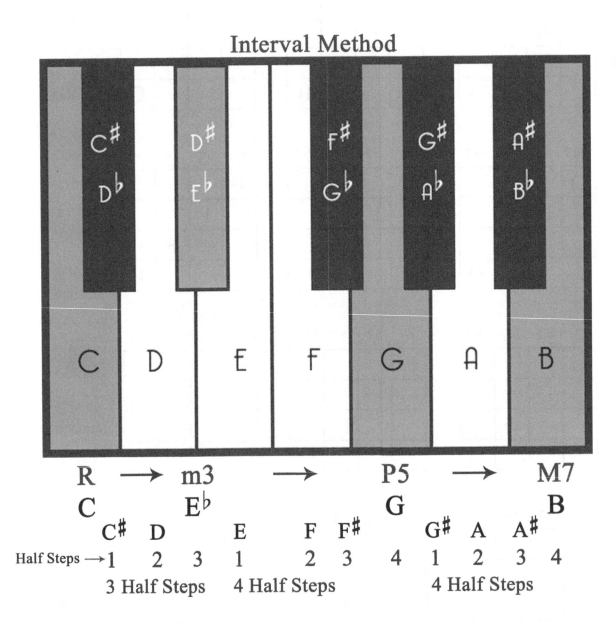

| R | → | m3 | → | P5 | → | M7 |
|---|---|----|----|----|----|----|
| C | | E♭ | | G | | B |

C#  D  E  F  F#  G#  A  A#

Half Steps → 1  2  3  1  2  3  4  1  2  3  4

3 Half Steps    4 Half Steps    4 Half Steps

# Minor Major 7ᵗʰ Chord

| R | ♭3 | 5 | 7 |
|---|---|---|---|
| A |  |  |  |
|  | A |  |  |
|  |  | A |  |
|  |  |  | A |

| R | ♭3 | 5 | 7 |
|---|---|---|---|
| B |  |  |  |
|  | B |  |  |
|  |  | B |  |
|  |  |  | B |

| R | ♭3 | 5 | 7 |
|---|---|---|---|
| C |  |  |  |
|  | C |  |  |
|  |  | C |  |
|  |  |  | C |

| R | ♭3 | 5 | 7 |
|---|---|---|---|
| D |  |  |  |
|  | D |  |  |
|  |  | D |  |
|  |  |  | D |

| R | ♭3 | 5 | 7 |
|---|---|---|---|
| E |  |  |  |
|  | E |  |  |
|  |  | E |  |
|  |  |  | E |

| R | ♭3 | 5 | 7 |
|---|---|---|---|
| F |  |  |  |
|  | F |  |  |
|  |  | F |  |
|  |  |  | F |

| R | ♭3 | 5 | 7 |
|---|---|---|---|
| G |  |  |  |
|  | G |  |  |
|  |  | G |  |
|  |  |  | G |

| R | ♭3 | 5 | 7 |
|---|---|---|---|
| F# |  |  |  |
|  | F# |  |  |
|  |  | F# |  |
|  |  |  | F# |

| R | ♭3 | 5 | 7 |
|---|---|---|---|
| C# |  |  |  |
|  | C# |  |  |
|  |  | C# |  |
|  |  |  | C# |

| R | ♭3 | 5 | 7 |
|---|---|---|---|
| E♭ |  |  |  |
|  | E♭ |  |  |
|  |  | E♭ |  |
|  |  |  | E♭ |

| R | ♭3 | 5 | 7 |
|---|---|---|---|
| A♭ |  |  |  |
|  | A♭ |  |  |
|  |  | A♭ |  |
|  |  |  | A♭ |

| R | ♭3 | 5 | 7 |
|---|---|---|---|
| B♭ |  |  |  |
|  | B♭ |  |  |
|  |  | B♭ |  |
|  |  |  | B♭ |

# Un-organized!
## All previous 4 note chords.
Check **page 50** if you're unsure how to do these puzzles. The same concept applies.

| 5 | R | 7 | 3 |
|---|---|---|---|
| C |   |   |   |
|   | C |   |   |
|   |   | C |   |
|   |   |   | C |

| R | ♭7 | 3 | 5 |
|---|----|---|---|
| G |    |   |   |
|   |    | G |   |
|   |    |   | G |
|   |    |   | G |

| 5 | R | ♭7 | 4 |
|---|---|----|---|
| D |   |    |   |
|   | D |    |   |
|   |   | D  |   |
|   |   |    | D |

| ♭3 | R | 7 | 5 |
|----|---|---|---|
| A  |   |   |   |
|    | A |   |   |
|    |   | A |   |
|    |   |   | A |

| R | ♭3 | ♭7 | ♭5 |
|---|----|----|----|
| E |    |    |    |
|   | E  |    |    |
|   |    | E  |    |
|   |    |    | E  |

| ♭5 | R | ♭3 | ♭♭7 |
|----|---|----|-----|
| B  |   |    |     |
|    | B |    |     |
|    |   | B  |     |
|    |   |    | B   |

| 7 | ♭3 | R | 5 |
|---|----|---|---|
| F# |   |   |   |
|   | F# |   |   |
|   |    | F# |  |
|   |    |   | F# |

| 5 | R | 3 | 6 |
|---|---|---|---|
| F |   |   |   |
|   | F |   |   |
|   |   | F |   |
|   |   |   | F |

| ♭3 | 6 | R | 5 |
|----|---|---|---|
| B♭ |   |   |   |
|    | B♭ |  |   |
|    |   | B♭ |  |
|    |   |   | B♭ |

| 5 | 3 | 7 | R |
|---|---|---|---|
| E♭ |  |   |   |
|   | E♭ |  |   |
|   |   | E♭ |  |
|   |   |   | E♭ |

| R | 5 | 3 | ♭7 |
|---|---|---|----|
| A♭ |  |   |    |
|   | A♭ |  |    |
|   |   | A♭ |   |
|   |   |   | A♭ |

| ♭7 | 5 | 4 | R |
|----|---|---|---|
| D♭ |  |   |   |
|    | D♭ |  |   |
|    |   | D♭ |  |
|    |   |   | D♭ |

# Un-organized 4 Note Chords/Arpeggios

**♭3  5  R  ♭7**

| C |  |  |  |
|---|---|---|---|
|  | C |  |  |
|  |  | C |  |
|  |  |  | C |

**♭7  ♭3  ♭5  R**

| G |  |  |  |
|---|---|---|---|
|  | G |  |  |
|  |  | G |  |
|  |  |  | G |

**R  ♭♭7  ♭3  ♭5**

| D |  |  |  |
|---|---|---|---|
|  |  | D |  |
|  |  |  | D |
|  |  |  | D |

**R  6  3  5**

| A |  |  |  |
|---|---|---|---|
|  | A |  |  |
|  |  | A |  |
|  |  |  | A |

**5  R  6  3**

| E |  |  |  |
|---|---|---|---|
|  | E |  |  |
|  |  | E |  |
|  |  |  | E |

**R  ♭3  5  6**

| B |  |  |  |
|---|---|---|---|
|  | B |  |  |
|  |  | B |  |
|  |  |  | B |

**3  5  7  R**

| F# |  |  |  |
|---|---|---|---|
|  | F# |  |  |
|  |  | F# |  |
|  |  |  | F# |

**5  ♭7  3  R**

| F |  |  |  |
|---|---|---|---|
|  | F |  |  |
|  |  | F |  |
|  |  |  | F |

**♭7  R  4  5**

| B♭ |  |  |  |
|---|---|---|---|
|  | B♭ |  |  |
|  |  | B♭ |  |
|  |  |  | B♭ |

**5  3  7  R**

| E♭ |  |  |  |
|---|---|---|---|
|  | E♭ |  |  |
|  |  | E♭ |  |
|  |  |  | E♭ |

**R  ♭7  ♭5  ♭3**

| A♭ |  |  |  |
|---|---|---|---|
|  | A♭ |  |  |
|  |  | A♭ |  |
|  |  |  | A♭ |

**♭♭7  ♭5  ♭3  R**

| D♭ |  |  |  |
|---|---|---|---|
|  | D♭ |  |  |
|  |  | D♭ |  |
|  |  |  | D♭ |

# Un-organized 4 Note Chords/Arpeggios

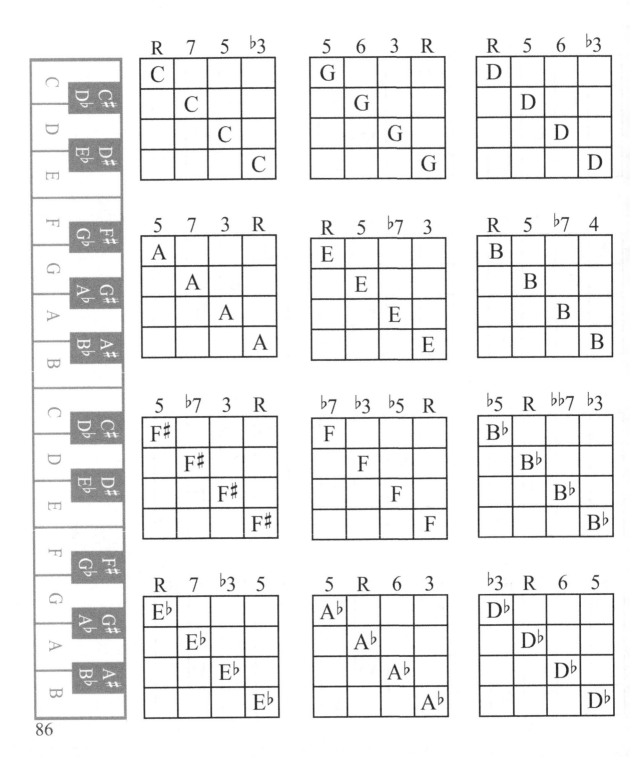

# Part IV
# SCALE PUZZLES

# Scale Puzzles

You will be working with 6 types of scales in this book. The scale puzzles work just like the chord/arpeggio puzzles. Make sure you have read pages 15-18 and have also done the scale sheets on pages 19-23 before doing this section of the book. That should clear up questions about the scales if you have any.

Here is a chart showing the 6 scales and their "building blocks."

| Scale Type | Scale Formula | Corresponding Scale Degrees |
|---|---|---|
| Major Pentatonic | W W W+½ W W+½ | 1 2 3 5 6 (8) |
| Minor Pentatonic | W+½ W W W+½ W | 1 2 ♭3 5 ♭7 (8) |
| Major (Ionian) | W W H W W W H | 1 2 3 4 5 6 7 (8) |
| Natural Minor | W H W W W H W | 1 2 ♭3 4 5 6 ♭7 (8) |
| Harmonic Minor | W H W W W+½ H W | 1 2 ♭3 4 5 ♭6 7 (8) |
| Melodic Minor (Jazz minor) | W H W W W W H | 1 2 ♭3 4 5 6 7 (8) |

Each page has a reminder/example of the elements in the scale you will be working on, just like the chord puzzles have. Again, I strongly recommend filling in the boxes and then checking answers on your instrument. Listen to what each scale sounds like. Make your own explanation for the sound that each scale creates if you want to. That way you really know the sound and can use it when that particular "spice" is needed in the mix.

# The Major Pentatonic Scale

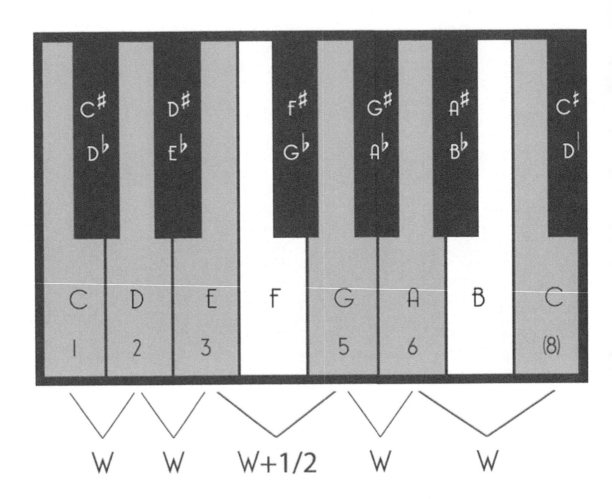

# Major Pentatonic

**A**

| R | 2 | 3 | 5 | 6 |
|---|---|---|---|---|
| A |   |   |   |   |
|   | A |   |   |   |
|   |   | A |   |   |
|   |   |   | A |   |
|   |   |   |   | A |

**D**

| R | 2 | 3 | 5 | 6 |
|---|---|---|---|---|
| D |   |   |   |   |
|   | D |   |   |   |
|   |   | D |   |   |
|   |   |   | D |   |
|   |   |   |   | D |

**B♭**

| R | 2 | 3 | 5 | 6 |
|---|---|---|---|---|
| B♭ |   |   |   |   |
|   | B♭ |   |   |   |
|   |   | B♭ |   |   |
|   |   |   | B♭ |   |
|   |   |   |   | B♭ |

**E♭**

| R | 2 | 3 | 5 | 6 |
|---|---|---|---|---|
| E♭ |   |   |   |   |
|   | E♭ |   |   |   |
|   |   | E♭ |   |   |
|   |   |   | E♭ |   |
|   |   |   |   | E♭ |

**G**

| R | 2 | 3 | 5 | 6 |
|---|---|---|---|---|
| G |   |   |   |   |
|   | G |   |   |   |
|   |   | G |   |   |
|   |   |   | G |   |
|   |   |   |   | G |

**C**

| R | 2 | 3 | 5 | 6 |
|---|---|---|---|---|
| C |   |   |   |   |
|   | C |   |   |   |
|   |   | C |   |   |
|   |   |   | C |   |
|   |   |   |   | C |

**A♭**

| R | 2 | 3 | 5 | 6 |
|---|---|---|---|---|
| A♭ |   |   |   |   |
|   | A♭ |   |   |   |
|   |   | A♭ |   |   |
|   |   |   | A♭ |   |
|   |   |   |   | A♭ |

**D♭**

| R | 2 | 3 | 5 | 6 |
|---|---|---|---|---|
| D♭ |   |   |   |   |
|   | D♭ |   |   |   |
|   |   | D♭ |   |   |
|   |   |   | D♭ |   |
|   |   |   |   | D♭ |

**F**

| R | 2 | 3 | 5 | 6 |
|---|---|---|---|---|
| F |   |   |   |   |
|   | F |   |   |   |
|   |   | F |   |   |
|   |   |   | F |   |
|   |   |   |   | F |

**B**

| R | 2 | 3 | 5 | 6 |
|---|---|---|---|---|
| B |   |   |   |   |
|   | B |   |   |   |
|   |   | B |   |   |
|   |   |   | B |   |
|   |   |   |   | B |

**E**

| R | 2 | 3 | 5 | 6 |
|---|---|---|---|---|
| E |   |   |   |   |
|   | E |   |   |   |
|   |   | E |   |   |
|   |   |   | E |   |
|   |   |   |   | E |

**G♭**

| R | 2 | 3 | 5 | 6 |
|---|---|---|---|---|
| G♭ |   |   |   |   |
|   | G♭ |   |   |   |
|   |   | G♭ |   |   |
|   |   |   | G♭ |   |
|   |   |   |   | G♭ |

Piano keyboard reference:

Black keys: C#/D♭, D#/E♭, F#/G♭, G#/A♭, A#/B♭, C#/D♭, D#/E♭, F#/G♭, G#/A♭, A#/B♭

White keys: C D E F G A B C D E F G A B

# The Minor Pentatonic Scale

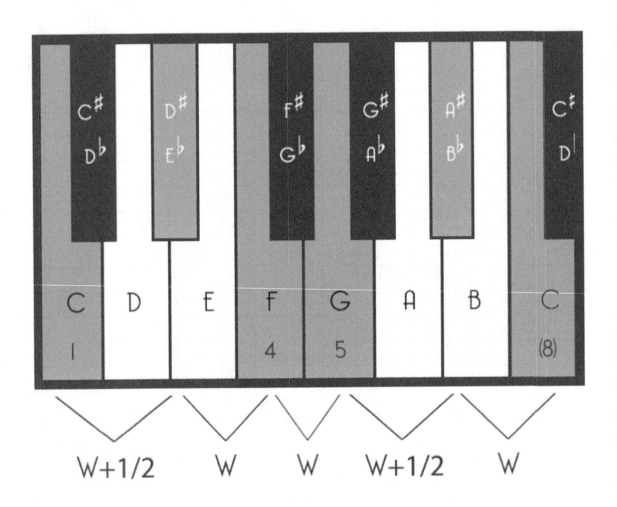

# Minor Pentatonic

**D**

| R | ♭3 | 4 | 5 | ♭7 |
|---|----|---|---|----|
| D |   |   |   |   |
|   | D |   |   |   |
|   |   | D |   |   |
|   |   |   | D |   |
|   |   |   |   | D |

**A**

| R | ♭3 | 4 | 5 | ♭7 |
|---|----|---|---|----|
| A |   |   |   |   |
|   | A |   |   |   |
|   |   | A |   |   |
|   |   |   | A |   |
|   |   |   |   | A |

**F**

| R | ♭3 | 4 | 5 | ♭7 |
|---|----|---|---|----|
| F |   |   |   |   |
|   | F |   |   |   |
|   |   | F |   |   |
|   |   |   | F |   |
|   |   |   |   | F |

**E**

| R | ♭3 | 4 | 5 | ♭7 |
|---|----|---|---|----|
| E |   |   |   |   |
|   | E |   |   |   |
|   |   | E |   |   |
|   |   |   | E |   |
|   |   |   |   | E |

**C**

| R | ♭3 | 4 | 5 | ♭7 |
|---|----|---|---|----|
| C |   |   |   |   |
|   | C |   |   |   |
|   |   | C |   |   |
|   |   |   | C |   |
|   |   |   |   | C |

**B♭**

| R | ♭3 | 4 | 5 | ♭7 |
|---|----|---|---|----|
| B♭ |   |   |   |   |
|   | B♭ |   |   |   |
|   |   | B♭ |   |   |
|   |   |   | B♭ |   |
|   |   |   |   | B♭ |

**E♭**

| R | ♭3 | 4 | 5 | ♭7 |
|---|----|---|---|----|
| E♭ |   |   |   |   |
|   | E♭ |   |   |   |
|   |   | E♭ |   |   |
|   |   |   | E♭ |   |
|   |   |   |   | E♭ |

**G**

| R | ♭3 | 4 | 5 | ♭7 |
|---|----|---|---|----|
| G |   |   |   |   |
|   | G |   |   |   |
|   |   | G |   |   |
|   |   |   | G |   |
|   |   |   |   | G |

**D♭**

| R | ♭3 | 4 | 5 | ♭7 |
|---|----|---|---|----|
| D♭ |   |   |   |   |
|   | D♭ |   |   |   |
|   |   | D♭ |   |   |
|   |   |   | D♭ |   |
|   |   |   |   | D♭ |

**B**

| R | ♭3 | 4 | 5 | ♭7 |
|---|----|---|---|----|
| B |   |   |   |   |
|   | B |   |   |   |
|   |   | B |   |   |
|   |   |   | B |   |
|   |   |   |   | B |

**A♭**

| R | ♭3 | 4 | 5 | ♭7 |
|---|----|---|---|----|
| A♭ |   |   |   |   |
|   | A♭ |   |   |   |
|   |   | A♭ |   |   |
|   |   |   | A♭ |   |
|   |   |   |   | A♭ |

**G♭**

| R | ♭3 | 4 | 5 | ♭7 |
|---|----|---|---|----|
| G♭ |   |   |   |   |
|   | G♭ |   |   |   |
|   |   | G♭ |   |   |
|   |   |   | G♭ |   |
|   |   |   |   | G♭ |

# The Major Scale
## (Ionian)

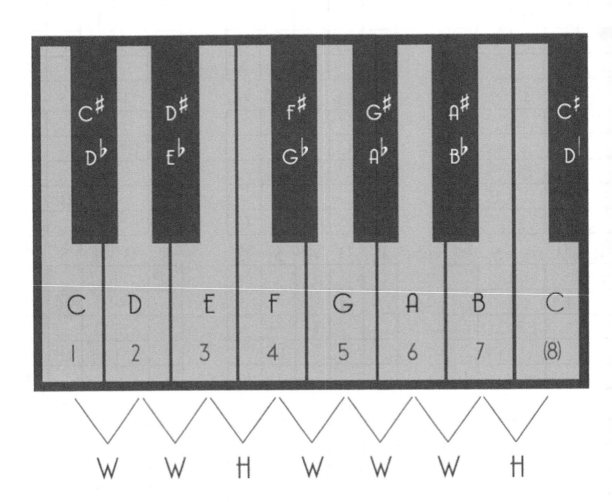

# The Major Scale
## (Ionian)

| R | 2 | 3 | 4 | 5 | 6 | 7 |
|---|---|---|---|---|---|---|
| F |   |   |   |   |   |   |
|   | F |   |   |   |   |   |
|   |   | F |   |   |   |   |
|   |   |   | F |   |   |   |
|   |   |   |   | F |   |   |
|   |   |   |   |   | F |   |
|   |   |   |   |   |   | F |

| R | 2 | 3 | 4 | 5 | 6 | 7 |
|---|---|---|---|---|---|---|
| D |   |   |   |   |   |   |
|   | D |   |   |   |   |   |
|   |   | D |   |   |   |   |
|   |   |   | D |   |   |   |
|   |   |   |   | D |   |   |
|   |   |   |   |   | D |   |
|   |   |   |   |   |   | D |

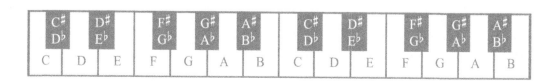

# The Major Scale
# (Ionian)

| R | 2 | 3 | 4 | 5 | 6 | 7 |
|---|---|---|---|---|---|---|
| B♭ | | | | | | |
| | B♭ | | | | | |
| | | B♭ | | | | |
| | | | B♭ | | | |
| | | | | B♭ | | |
| | | | | | B♭ | |
| | | | | | | B♭ |

| R | 2 | 3 | 4 | 5 | 6 | 7 |
|---|---|---|---|---|---|---|
| A | | | | | | |
| | A | | | | | |
| | | A | | | | |
| | | | A | | | |
| | | | | A | | |
| | | | | | A | |
| | | | | | | A |

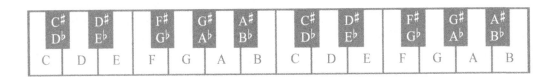

# The Major Scale
## (Ionian)

| R | 2 | 3 | 4 | 5 | 6 | 7 |
|---|---|---|---|---|---|---|
| F# | | | | | | |
| | F# | | | | | |
| | | F# | | | | |
| | | | F# | | | |
| | | | | F# | | |
| | | | | | F# | |
| | | | | | | F# |

| R | 2 | 3 | 4 | 5 | 6 | 7 |
|---|---|---|---|---|---|---|
| E♭ | | | | | | |
| | E♭ | | | | | |
| | | E♭ | | | | |
| | | | E♭ | | | |
| | | | | E♭ | | |
| | | | | | E♭ | |
| | | | | | | E♭ |

| C# / D♭ | D# / E♭ | | F# / G♭ | G# / A♭ | A# / B♭ | | C# / D♭ | D# / E♭ | | F# / G♭ | G# / A♭ | A# / B♭ |
|---|---|---|---|---|---|---|---|---|---|---|---|---|
| C | D | E | F | G | A | B | C | D | E | F | G | A | B |

# The Natural Minor Scale

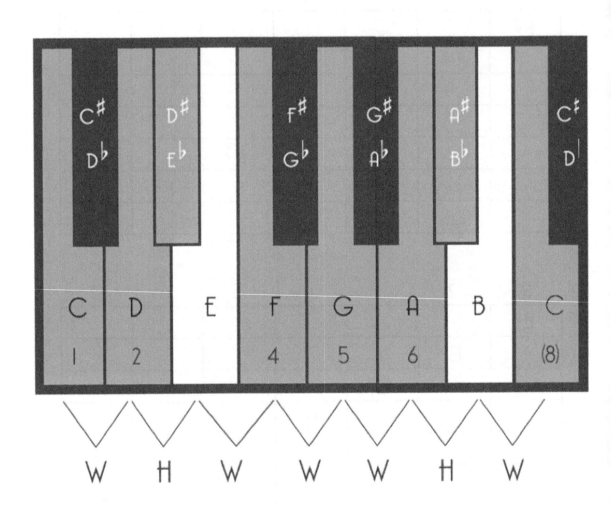

# The Natural Minor Scale

| R | 2 | ♭3 | 4 | 5 | ♭6 | ♭7 |
|---|---|----|---|---|----|----|
| A |   |    |   |   |    |    |
|   | A |    |   |   |    |    |
|   |   | A  |   |   |    |    |
|   |   |    | A |   |    |    |
|   |   |    |   | A |    |    |
|   |   |    |   |   | A  |    |
|   |   |    |   |   |    | A  |

| R | 2 | ♭3 | 4 | 5 | ♭6 | ♭7 |
|---|---|----|---|---|----|----|
| C |   |    |   |   |    |    |
|   | C |    |   |   |    |    |
|   |   | C  |   |   |    |    |
|   |   |    | C |   |    |    |
|   |   |    |   | C |    |    |
|   |   |    |   |   | C  |    |
|   |   |    |   |   |    | C  |

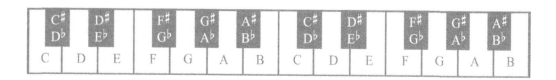

# The Natural Minor Scale

| R | 2 | ♭3 | 4 | 5 | ♭6 | ♭7 |
|---|---|---|---|---|---|---|
| F |   |   |   |   |   |   |
|   | F |   |   |   |   |   |
|   |   | F |   |   |   |   |
|   |   |   | F |   |   |   |
|   |   |   |   | F |   |   |
|   |   |   |   |   | F |   |
|   |   |   |   |   |   | F |

| R | 2 | ♭3 | 4 | 5 | ♭6 | ♭7 |
|---|---|---|---|---|---|---|
| G |   |   |   |   |   |   |
|   | G |   |   |   |   |   |
|   |   | G |   |   |   |   |
|   |   |   | G |   |   |   |
|   |   |   |   | G |   |   |
|   |   |   |   |   | G |   |
|   |   |   |   |   |   | G |

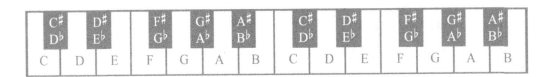

# The Natural Minor Scale

| R | 2 | ♭3 | 4 | 5 | ♭6 | ♭7 |
|---|---|----|---|---|----|----|
| E♭ | | | | | | |
| | E♭ | | | | | |
| | | E♭ | | | | |
| | | | E♭ | | | |
| | | | | E♭ | | |
| | | | | | E♭ | |
| | | | | | | E♭ |

| R | 2 | ♭3 | 4 | 5 | ♭6 | ♭7 |
|---|---|----|---|---|----|----|
| A♭ | | | | | | |
| | A♭ | | | | | |
| | | A♭ | | | | |
| | | | A♭ | | | |
| | | | | A♭ | | |
| | | | | | A♭ | |
| | | | | | | A♭ |

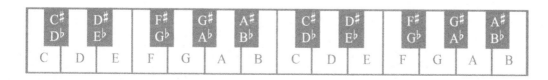

# The Harmonic Minor Scale

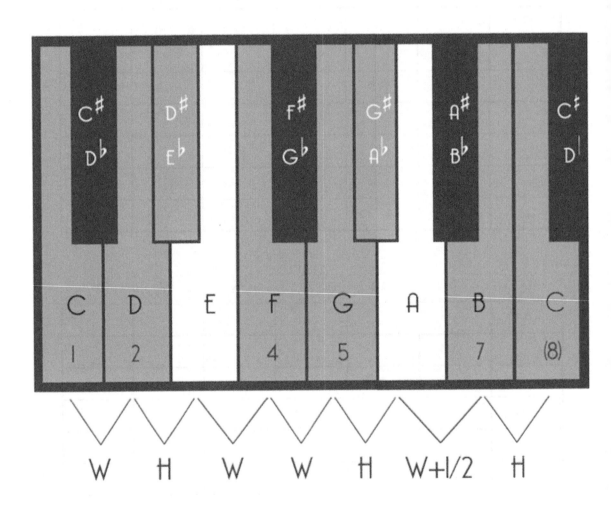

# The Harmonic Minor Scale

| R | 2 | ♭3 | 4 | 5 | ♭6 | 7 |
|---|---|---|---|---|---|---|
| C | | | | | | |
| | C | | | | | |
| | | C | | | | |
| | | | C | | | |
| | | | | C | | |
| | | | | | C | |
| | | | | | | C |

| R | 2 | ♭3 | 4 | 5 | ♭6 | 7 |
|---|---|---|---|---|---|---|
| G | | | | | | |
| | G | | | | | |
| | | G | | | | |
| | | | G | | | |
| | | | | G | | |
| | | | | | G | |
| | | | | | | G |

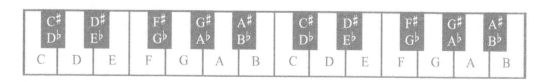

# The Harmonic Minor Scale

| R | 2 | ♭3 | 4 | 5 | ♭6 | 7 |
|---|---|---|---|---|---|---|
| B |   |   |   |   |   |   |
|   | B |   |   |   |   |   |
|   |   | B |   |   |   |   |
|   |   |   | B |   |   |   |
|   |   |   |   | B |   |   |
|   |   |   |   |   | B |   |
|   |   |   |   |   |   | B |

| R | 2 | ♭3 | 4 | 5 | ♭6 | 7 |
|---|---|---|---|---|---|---|
| D |   |   |   |   |   |   |
|   | D |   |   |   |   |   |
|   |   | D |   |   |   |   |
|   |   |   | D |   |   |   |
|   |   |   |   | D |   |   |
|   |   |   |   |   | D |   |
|   |   |   |   |   |   | D |

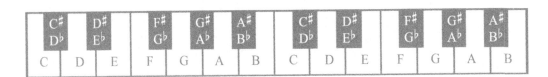

# The Harmonic Minor Scale

| R | 2 | ♭3 | 4 | 5 | ♭6 | 7 |
|---|---|----|---|---|----|---|
| E |   |    |   |   |    |   |
|   | E |    |   |   |    |   |
|   |   | E  |   |   |    |   |
|   |   |    | E |   |    |   |
|   |   |    |   | E |    |   |
|   |   |    |   |   | E  |   |
|   |   |    |   |   |    | E |

| R | 2 | ♭3 | 4 | 5 | ♭6 | 7 |
|---|---|----|---|---|----|---|
| D♭ |   |    |   |   |    |   |
|   | D♭ |    |   |   |    |   |
|   |   | D♭ |   |   |    |   |
|   |   |    | D♭ |   |    |   |
|   |   |    |   | D♭ |    |   |
|   |   |    |   |   | D♭ |   |
|   |   |    |   |   |    | D♭ |

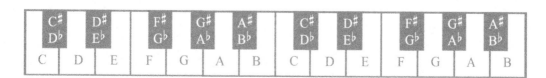

# The Melodic Minor Scale
## (The "Jazz Minor" Scale)

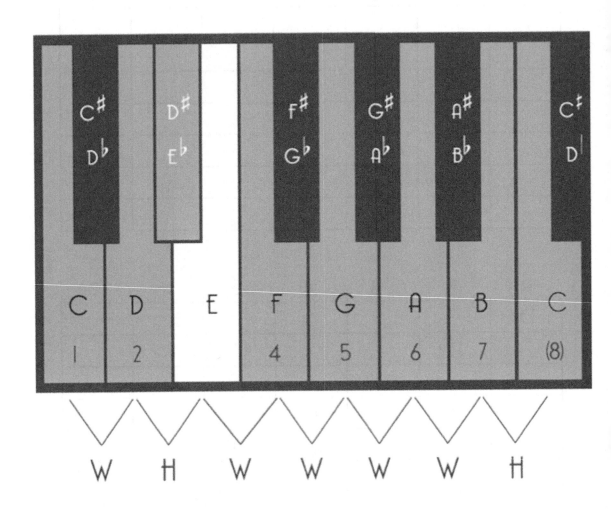

# The Melodic Minor Scale

| R | 2 | ♭3 | 4 | 5 | 6 | 7 |
|---|---|----|---|---|---|---|
| B |   |    |   |   |   |   |
|   | B |    |   |   |   |   |
|   |   | B  |   |   |   |   |
|   |   |    | B |   |   |   |
|   |   |    |   | B |   |   |
|   |   |    |   |   | B |   |
|   |   |    |   |   |   | B |

| R | 2 | ♭3 | 4 | 5 | 6 | 7 |
|---|---|----|---|---|---|---|
| F♯ |   |    |   |   |   |   |
|   | F♯ |    |   |   |   |   |
|   |   | F♯ |   |   |   |   |
|   |   |    | F♯ |   |   |   |
|   |   |    |   | F♯ |   |   |
|   |   |    |   |   | F♯ |   |
|   |   |    |   |   |   | F♯ |

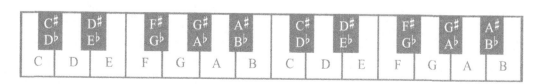

# The Melodic Minor Scale
## (The "Jazz Minor" Scale)

| R | 2 | ♭3 | 4 | 5 | 6 | 7 |
|---|---|---|---|---|---|---|
| A |   |   |   |   |   |   |
|   | A |   |   |   |   |   |
|   |   | A |   |   |   |   |
|   |   |   | A |   |   |   |
|   |   |   |   | A |   |   |
|   |   |   |   |   | A |   |
|   |   |   |   |   |   | A |

| R | 2 | ♭3 | 4 | 5 | 6 | 7 |
|---|---|---|---|---|---|---|
| B♭ |   |   |   |   |   |   |
|   | B♭ |   |   |   |   |   |
|   |   | B♭ |   |   |   |   |
|   |   |   | B♭ |   |   |   |
|   |   |   |   | B♭ |   |   |
|   |   |   |   |   | B♭ |   |
|   |   |   |   |   |   | B♭ |

# The Melodic Minor Scale

| R | 2 | b3 | 4 | 5 | 6 | 7 |
|---|---|---|---|---|---|---|
| G# | | | | | | |
| | G# | | | | | |
| | | G# | | | | |
| | | | G# | | | |
| | | | | G# | | |
| | | | | | G# | |
| | | | | | | G# |

| R | 2 | b3 | 4 | 5 | 6 | 7 |
|---|---|---|---|---|---|---|
| D# | | | | | | |
| | D# | | | | | |
| | | D# | | | | |
| | | | D# | | | |
| | | | | D# | | |
| | | | | | D# | |
| | | | | | | D# |

| C#/Db | D#/Eb | | F#/Gb | G#/Ab | A#/Bb | | C#/Db | D#/Eb | | F#/Gb | G#/Ab | A#/Bb | |
|---|---|---|---|---|---|---|---|---|---|---|---|---|---|
| C | D | E | F | G | A | B | C | D | E | F | G | A | B |

| | | | | | | | | |
|---|---|---|---|---|---|---|---|---|
| (1 HS) **mi2** | A - *B♭* | B - *C* | C - *D♭* | D - *E♭* | E - *F* | F - *G♭* | G - *A♭* | A - *B♭* |
| (2 HS) **MA2** | B - *C#* | C - *D* | D - *E* | E - *F#* | F - *G* | G - *A* | A - *B* | B - *C#* |
| (3 HS) **mi3** | C - *E♭* | D - *F* | E - *G* | F - *A♭* | G - *B♭* | A - *C* | B - *D* | C - *E♭* |
| (4 HS) **MA3** | D - *F#* | E - *G#* | F - *A* | G - *B* | A - *C#* | B - *D#* | C - *E* | D - *F#* |
| (5 HS) **P4** | E - *A* | F - *B♭* | G - *C* | A - *D* | B - *E* | C - *F* | D - *G* | E - *A* |
| (6 HS) **A4** | F - *B* | G - *C#* | A - *D#* | B - *E#* | C - *F#* | D - *G#* | E - *A#* | F - *B* |
| (6 HS) **dim5** | G - *D♭* | A - *E♭* | B - *F* | C - *G♭* | D - *A♭* | E - *B♭* | F - *C♭* | G - *D♭* |
| (7 HS) **P5** | A - *E* | B - *F#* | C - *G* | D - *A* | E - *B* | F - *C* | G - *D* | A - *E* |
| (8 HS) **A5** | B - *F×* | C - *G#* | D - *A#* | E - *B#* | F - *C#* | G - *D#* | A - *E#* | B - *F×* |
| (8 HS) **mi6** | C - *A♭* | D - *B♭* | E - *C* | F - *D♭* | G - *E♭* | A - *F* | B - *G* | C - *A♭* |
| (9 HS) **MA6** | D - *B* | E - *C#* | F - *D* | G - *E* | A - *F#* | B - *G#* | C - *A* | D - *B* |
| (9 HS) **dim7** | E - *D♭* | F - *E♭♭* | G - *F♭* | A - *G♭* | B - *A♭* | C - *B♭♭* | D - *C♭* | E - *D♭* |
| (10 HS) **mi7** | F - *E♭* | G - *A* | A - *G* | B - *A* | C - *B♭* | D - *C* | E - *D* | F - *E♭* |
| (11 HS) **MA7** | G - *F#* | A - *G#* | B - *A#* | C - *B* | D - *C#* | E - *D#* | F - *E* | G - *F#* |
| (12 HS) **P8** | A - *A* | B - *B* | C - *C* | D - *D* | E - *E* | F - *F* | G - *G* | A - *A* |

| Do | Re | Mi | Fa | Sol | La | Ti | (Do) |
|----|----|----|----|-----|----|----|------|
| 1  | 2  | 3  | 4  | 5   | 6  | 7  | (8)  |
| R  | W  | W  | H  | W   | W  | W  | H    |
| C  | D  | E  | F  | G   | A  | B  | C    |
| G  | A  | B  | C  | D   | E  | F♯ | G    |
| D  | E  | F♯ | G  | A   | B  | C♯ | D    |
| A  | B  | C♯ | D  | E   | F♯ | G♯ | A    |
| E  | F♯ | G♯ | A  | B   | C♯ | D♯ | E    |
| B  | C♯ | D♯ | E  | F♯  | G♯ | A♯ | B    |
| F♯ | G♯ | A♯ | B  | C♯  | D♯ | E♯ | F♯   |
| C♯ | D♯ | E♯ | F♯ | G♯  | A♯ | B♯ | C♯   |
| F  | G  | A  | B♭ | C   | D  | E  | F    |
| B♭ | C  | D  | E♭ | F   | G  | A  | B♭   |
| E♭ | F  | G  | A♭ | B♭  | C  | D  | E♭   |
| A♭ | B♭ | C  | D♭ | E♭  | F  | G  | A♭   |
| D♭ | E♭ | F  | G♭ | A♭  | B♭ | C  | D♭   |
| G♭ | A♭ | B♭ | C♭ | D♭  | E♭ | F  | G♭   |
| C♭ | D♭ | E♭ | F♭ | G♭  | A♭ | B♭ | C♭   |

Made in the USA
Coppell, TX
12 March 2024

30040369R00063